GALLIPOLI
ONE LONG GRAVE

A group of Anzacs examine a captured Turkish trench at Lone Pine. The covered and heavily timbered trenches of the Turks were more solidly fortified than the Anzacs' initial positions.

GALLIPOLI
ONE LONG GRAVE

KIT DENTON

TIME-LIFE BOOKS. AUSTRALIA
in association with JOHN FERGUSON. SYDNEY

Designed and produced by
John Ferguson Pty Ltd
100 Kippax Street,
Surry Hills, NSW 2010

Series Editor: John Ferguson
Consulting Editor: George C. Daniels
Text Editor: Anthony Barker
Picture Editor: Elisa Clarke
Series Administrator: Lesley McKay
Production Manager: Ian MacArthur
Designer: Pamela Drewitt Smith
Concept Design: Hans Selhoffer
Assembly Artists: Derryn Tal, Josie Howlett

Time-Life Books, South Pacific Books Division
Managing Director: Bonita L. Boezeman
Production Manager: Ken G. Hiley

The Author: KIT DENTON is a freelance writer with a
special interest in military history. His own military service
was spent in the Royal Artillery and the Parachute Regiment
followed by a spell with the British forces radio network.
After coming to Australia in 1950, he worked for 15 years in
radio, mainly with the ABC, then as a freelance writer in
film, radio and television. Of his five published books, the
best known is *The Breaker,* the story of Breaker Morant.

First published in 1986 by
Time-Life Books (Australia) Pty Ltd
15 Blue Street
North Sydney, NSW 2060

National Library of Australia
cataloguing-in-publication data
Denton, Kit.
  Gallipoli, one long grave.

  Bibliography.
  Includes index.
  ISBN 0 949118 04 4.
  1. World War, 1914-1918 – Campaigns – Turkey – Gallipoli
Peninsula. I. Title. (Series: Australians at war; no. 1).

Printed in Hong Kong

CONTENTS

1

THE DARDANELLES: STRUGGLE AT SEA

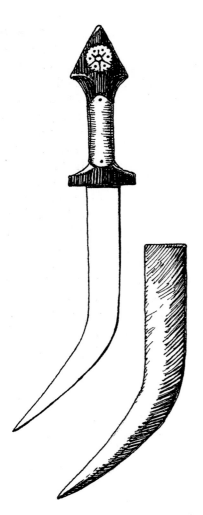

Turkish dagger.

The Dardanelles was strategically vital. Control of the waterway by the Allies would mean the opening of a supply line to Russia and the elimination of Turkey from the war. But two attempts by the Royal Navy ended in failure and tragic losses.

It flows for less than 65 kilometres and is never more than seven kilometres wide. At its narrowest it spans a bare kilometre and a half, and it runs only 60 metres deep. Its name is the Dardanelles, and in the spring of 1915 it was the most important stretch of water in the world. A narrow peninsula formed its western shore, and there stood the town of Gelibolu. Australian soldiers came to know it intimately. They called it Gallipoli.

The strategic importance of that strip of water separating Asia from Europe was plain to see. One end of it led through the Sea of Marmara to the inland expanse of the Black Sea; the other end led through the Aegean to the Mediterranean and so to the world. Control of the Dardanelles meant control of the only outlet from the great rivers Danube, Don, Dnieper and Dniester, meant control of the ports of Odessa, Sevastopol and Constantinople – known today as Istanbul. To the east stretched the bulk of Turkey's Ottoman Empire, and close by the western run of the waters were the shaky states of Bulgaria and Romania. Northwards was the vast sprawl of Russia, allied with Britain and France in the war that had already linked Switzerland to the North Sea by an open wound.

The Dardanelles ran through the heart of Turkey, and Turkey was an ally of Germany's in the Great War. To take those waters and hold them meant the opening of a vital supply link to embattled Russia, the reduction of Turkey as a threat to the Suez Canal and the neutralising of the Balkans. To some planners and politicians it seemed that a successful attack on the Dardanelles would link the separated Allies and make possible a conjunction of sorts between the Eastern and Western Fronts. If such an attack was successful, it would open a pipeline into Russia for men and munitions and possibly lay open the plains of Austria-Hungary to an assault on the German armies from the flank and the rear.

If it was successful.

A leading advocate of an attack in the east, Winston Churchill, was in an excellent position to advance its cause. As First Lord of the Admiralty, he was able to urge the War Council to respond to Russia's calls for relief by attacking the Central Powers through Turkey. Lord Kitchener, Secretary of State for War, while not overtly opposing any plan for a Dardanelles attack, made it plain that he would not weaken the Western Front by moving troops away from Europe. It was an attitude that did more than mark a difference of opinion between the polarised groupings becoming known as Easterners and Westerners. The ten-year-old Committee of Imperial Defence had been unable to consider properly combined operations because of the set attitudes which maintained an unhealthy rivalry—amounting to animosity—between the army and the navy. Kitchener, not openly supporting either Easterners or Westerners, nonetheless offered no practical military support to the proposal to take the war into Turkish territory. He suggested that the opening of the Dardanelles was a job for the Royal Navy alone.

However willing the navy may have been to go along with Churchill's ideas, there were plain facts that had to be faced. The waters in which they would have to fight were hardly conducive to naval manoeuvring; narrow and shallow, they were flanked on both sides by rising ground, and both land and water were not only enemy held but well fortified.

Churchill received two differing responses from the navy to the problem he had set them. From Admiral Lord "Jackie" Fisher, First Sea Lord, came the suggestion for a massive and widespread attack on Turkey involving a squadron of battleships supported by close to 100,000 British and Indian troops, plus additional Greek and Bulgarian forces. Vice-Admiral Sackville Carden, commanding the British squadron in the Aegean, was more sanguine, suggesting that the Dardanelles might be forced "by extended operations with large numbers of ships." Churchill, enthused by Carden's reply and conscious of Kitchener's reluctance to commit land forces, asked for detailed needs for forcing the Dardanelles with naval might alone. The admiral came back with a list which began with a dozen battleships, included a massive fleet of three battle-cruisers, 16 destroyers, six submarines, 12 minesweepers and auxiliaries, and ended with four seaplanes. Churchill managed not only to get Fisher to agree with Carden's plans but persuaded the First Sea Lord to add two more battleships to the proposed fleet. By the end of January 1915, an assault on the Dardanelles had become a reality. It was, until then, no more than a naval assault, although prudent military minds, Kitchener's not least among them, recognised the possible need for troops to hold what the navy might win.

On February 19, 1915, Admiral Carden took his fleet into the Dardanelles. There were now 18 battleships, mounting a vast array of guns ranging from 4-inch to 15-inch in size. It was the greatest assemblage of naval firepower ever seen till then. Four of the big ships were from a French squadron commanded by Admiral Émile Guépratte, and the fleet's minesweepers were manned almost entirely by civilians. This last was to prove an error of major proportions.

The attack began, as planned, with systematic shelling, gradually closing but not fully effective, and it became plain that each Turkish gun site would have to be engaged directly by 7 observed fire if the progress up the narrow waterway was to continue. The weather closed in, however, and there was almost a week's delay before the naval guns opened up again, this time hammering the outer forts into silence, their crews either dead or put to flight. Minesweepers pushed upstream against the current and cleared a 10-kilometre stretch, and marines and sailors were put ashore, meeting little resistance and destroying 50 guns.

The Turks, a little demoralised at first, were quick to recover. By March 4 they had reinforced the peninsula forts and those at Kum Kale on the Asian side, and the parties that landed there were repulsed with a number of casualties. By then the fleet was about halfway between the entrance to the Dardanelles and the Narrows, the gap about 1,600 metres wide between the fortifications at Kilid Bahr and Chanak. They were too far from the next com-plex of Turkish guns to engage them accurately, and the capricious weather made it impossible for the seaplanes of the fleet to fly spotting missions. It was time to push the minesweepers forward again, but they came under heavy gunfire, and the civilian crews complained that they had not been engaged to come under fire, only to sweep mines. They refused to go further till the batteries were silenced.

The problem for Admiral Carden was that his guns could not silence the Turkish batteries until the mined waters were cleared. It was a stalemate, and the Admiral was ill-equipped by temperament to deal with it. He had been indiscreet enough to advise London early in the attack that he expected to break through to the Sea of Marmara within two weeks; now, with no news of advances reaching him, Churchill began to harry Carden in urgent signals. That pressure, the continued delay in advancing and

A Turkish artist's impression of British and French warships under fire during the second naval assault on the Dardanelles.
The French battleship Bouvet is seen sinking.

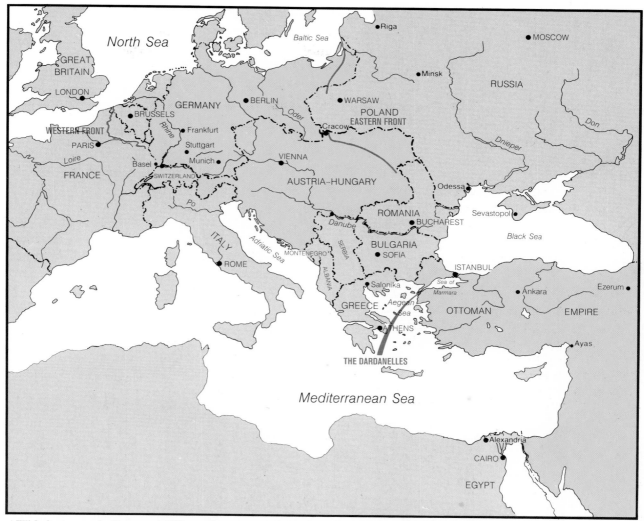

With the war on the Eastern and Western fronts at a stalemate in early 1915, an attack on the Dardanelles seemed likely to serve the triple purpose of diverting German forces from those fronts, eliminating Turkey from the war, and opening a supply line to Russia. Tinted areas on the map indicate the territory of the Central Powers; the broken boundary lines show the armistice line of November 1918.

the vagaries of the weather all preyed on Carden to the point where he was pronounced to be on the edge of a complete breakdown. He was ordered home. The command of the fleet passed to Vice-Admiral J.M. de Robeck, an excellent seaman, slow but resolute and fully committed to the Dardanelles operation. A month after the first assault, de Robeck took the fleet forward to attack the Narrows.

That day, March 18, 1915, saw a naval battle which could very easily have altered the whole course of the war. De Robeck's 14 battleships, reinforced a little after noon by Guépratte's French ships, battered their way towards the Narrows, 15-inch guns smashing into the forts there at long range. But those forts, built in

medieval times, were immensely thick-walled and solid, set into rock. To attack them successfully would have needed heavy and high-angled mortars or howitzers; the flat-trajectory naval guns had a comparatively minor effect.

As the shores closed towards the Narrows, the howitzers and mobile cannon on shore began to score damaging hits on the ships between them. The Turkish gunners, very well trained by their German instructors, kept up a rapid and accurate fire. Although their field guns were fairly small calibre, their howitzers and some heavy mortars ranged from 5.9-inch to 8-inch, and the dropping fire from them, combined with air-burst shrapnel, caused very considerable damage. More importantly, the constant

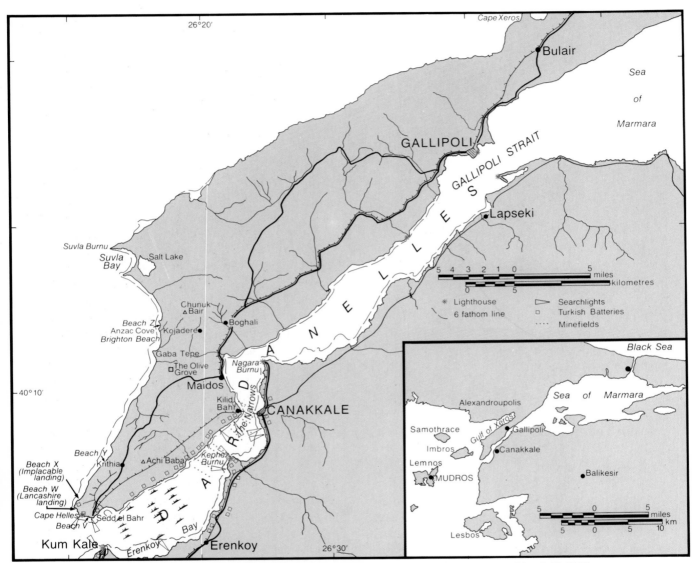

The Dardanelles and the Gallipoli peninsula, showing the sea attack on the Narrows on March 18, 1915.

fire tended to keep the Allied ships well offshore and force them into the areas that had been heavily sewn with mines. De Robeck signalled the French ships to withdraw as he was bringing up the rearmost line of British battleships. It was then, as the manoeuvre began in those constrained waters, that the drama of the action became a tragedy.

The French ship *Bouvet*, turning under fire, struck a mine. She was a 12,000-ton battleship, one of the old ships which preceded the Dreadnought type; the mine ruptured her 41-centimetre belt armour and she blew apart, going under almost at once and taking down almost all her crew of 600. That sight, plus the curtain of fire laid down by the Turkish howitzers, was enough to convince the civilian crews of the unarmoured minesweepers to turn and sail clear. As if to emphasise the point, HMS *Inflexible* ran onto a mine at almost the same spot as the French ship had done and began to list heavily. Not long after the *Bouvet* had gone down, HMS *Irresistible* struck the same minefield and was holed and unable to steer properly.

By the onset of dusk and with continued heavy firing from both ships and shore, it seemed to de Robeck that there was little more he could do. He was not to know that the Turkish guns were virtually out of ammunition and that a determined push, despite heavy losses, might well have carried them through. Churchill had signalled to Carden in the week before he had broken down, "The operation should now be pressed forward methodically and resolutely at night and day. The unavoidable losses must be accepted." Perhaps de Robeck had not seen that signal; perhaps he felt the losses had been too heavy. Whatever his reasons, he broke off the engagement and withdrew his battered fleet. To have pushed on, to have taken those "unavoidable losses", might well have given the Allies Constantinople and the seaway to Russia. With the Turkish capital in hand and an Allied fleet controlling the Dardanelles, it is likely that the government of the country would have yielded. Gallipoli might easily have become no more than a garrison area.

A week earlier, General Sir Ian Hamilton had been appointed to command the troops being assembled to exploit the hoped-for naval successes. Hamilton, 61 years old, was an intensely and devotedly professional soldier with a wealth of practical military knowledge. He had seen tough action against the Pathans in north-west India, served in administrative posts in Burma and Chitral, risked his life as an observer with the Japanese in Manchuria when they fought the Russians, and served in the Sudan and in South Africa during the Boer War, by which time he was chief of staff to Kitchener.

Hamilton was also a skilled and graceful writer, his literary ability being matched by acute – and frequently unpopular – military comment. Books in which he advocated radical changes in military attitudes drew a considerable amount of criticism from his fellows, and although he successfully held the post of General Officer Commanding Southern Command for several years, it seemed unlikely that he would achieve high command when the war broke out. It is virtually certain that the combination of his friendship with Winston Churchill and his past service with Kitchener gave him the command in the Dardanelles.

Hamilton was on hand to witness part of the sea battle on March 18. Another army observer was General William Birdwood, commander of the Australian and New Zealand forces he was training in Egypt for operations on the Western Front. Neither general was impressed with the handling of the naval fighting. The day after the battle, Hamilton signalled to Kitchener, "I am most reluctantly driven to the conclusion that the Straits are not likely to be forced by battleships, as at one time seemed probable, and that if my troops take part, it will not take the subsidiary form anticipated. It must be a deliberate and prepared military operation, carried out at full strength to open a passage for the navy." Kitchener's reply was prompt. "The Dardanelles must be forced, and if large military operations on the Gallipoli Peninsula are necessary to clear the way, those operations must be undertaken, after careful consideration of the local defences, and must be carried through."

Before a meeting with de Robeck and his staff, Hamilton, his Chief of Staff, General Walter Braithwaite, and Birdwood agreed that they would only talk about army operations if the Royal Navy actually asked for help. At that meeting on March 22, and despite his insistence right up to the start of the meeting, de Robeck suddenly changed his mind and said plainly that he was now quite clear that he could not get through the Dardanelles without military assistance. That was enough to tip the balance. The sea battle for the Dardanelles was over. The land battle was being primed to explode.

THE CHANCE OF A LIFETIME

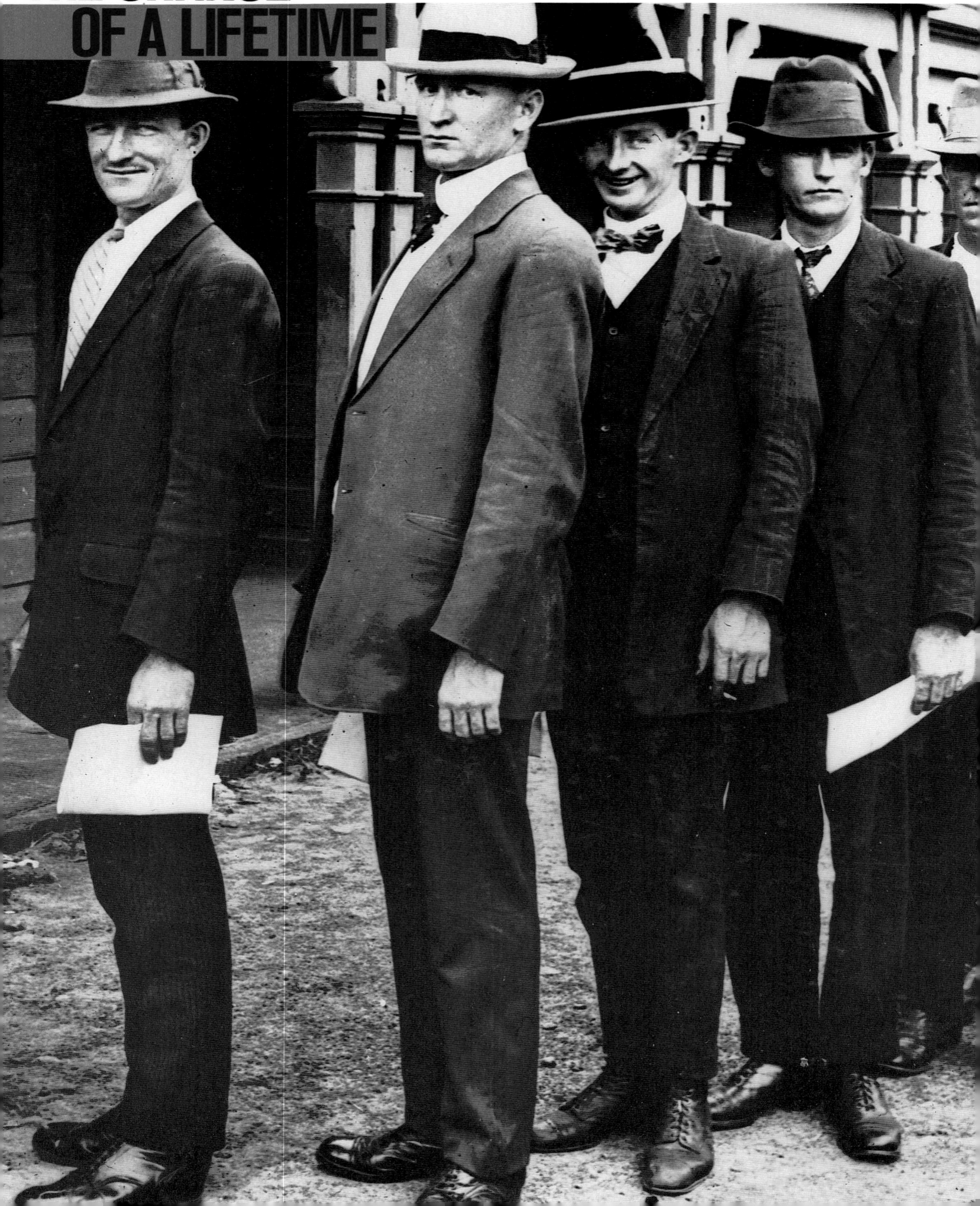

Volunteers queue up to enlist in Melbourne – influenced, perhaps, by the duplicity of the recruiting brochure.

Free Tour to Great Britain and Europe

THE CHANCE OF A LIFETIME

HOW TO JOIN THIS TOUR.

To participate in this unique offer, you must be between the ages of 18 and 45, have a minimum height of 5 feet 2 inches, and be able to expand your chest to 33 inches.

If you can meet these requirements fill in the application form hereunder, and post it to the Organising Secretary, State Recruiting Office, Sydney.

I hereby offer myself for enlistment in the Australian Imperial Force for active service abroad, and undertake to enlist in the manner prescribed, if I am accepted by the military authorities.

Age............ Height............ Weight............

Occupation ....

Signature ....

Postal Address ....

....

Date............
William Brooks & Co., Ltd., Printers, Sydney.

HOW YOU ARE PAID DAILY WHILE ON THIS TOUR.

Acting-Bombardier, Lance-Corporal Gunner, Sapper, Private, Bandsman, Collarmaker, Saddler, Wheeler, Trumpeter, Bugler, Drummer, Cook, Batman, ... 6/-
Stretcher-bearer ... 7/-
1/- deferred.
Shoeing Smith and Driver ... 6/-
1/- deferred.
Cleaners and Waggonmen (Mechanical Transport) ...
1/- deferred.

Mechanical Transport—Workshop Fitters, Turners, Blacksmiths, Wheelers, Electricians, and Drivers (Flying Unit and A.M.C. ... 8/-
Mechanics (Flying Unit and Motor Lorries) ... 9/-
1/6 deferred.

2nd Corporal Bombardier ... 10/-
1/6 deferred.
Corporal, Armourer, Band, Shoeing-smith, Signalling or Pay and Orderly-room Corporal ...
1/6 deferred.

Sergeant, Pioneer, Signalling, Transport, Armourer, or Band-Sergeant, Sergeant-Trumpeter ... 10/6
2/- deferred.

Squadron, Battery, Troop, or Company Quartermaster-Sergeant, Orderly-room Sergeant, Farrier, Collarmaker, Wheeler, or Saddler-Sergeant, or Sergeants of Mechanical Transport and Flying Units ... 11/6
2/- deferred.

Staff-Sergeant-Major, Squadron, Battery, Troop, or Company Sergeant-Major, Farrier Quartermaster-Sergeant, Quartermaster-Sergeant (Flying Unit), Colour-Sergeant, Staff-Sergeant, Armourer Staff-Sergeant, Sergeant-Cook, Wheeler, Staff-Sergeant ... 12/-
2/6 deferred. ... 14/-

Staff-Sergeant (Wireless)
Brigade or Regimental Sergeant-Major, Quartermaster-Sergeant, Armament Artificer, Sergeant Artificer (Mechanical Transport), Foreman Artificer Mechanic (Flying Unit), Warrant Officer ... 13/-
2/6 deferred. ... 21/-

Lieutenant, 2nd Lieutenant ... 3/- deferred.

SEPARATION ALLOWANCES:

Dependents of members of the A.I.F. receiving less than 10/- per diem (including deferred pay after embarkation) will be entitled to receive separation allowance on and from the 1st July, 1917, for each day for which pay is due under the following conditions subject to relative instructions which have, or may be issued, with additional payment from Lord Mayor's Fund (see below).

For wife living at home, irrespective of any private income now existing or subsequently arising—1/5 per diem.

For each child under 16 years of age—4½d. per diem.

For mothers dependent, or partly dependent, on soldier at time of enlistment, at same rate and under same conditions as wives, when not in receipt of invalid, old age or war pension.

For mothers, who are not, at time of son's enlistment, solely or partly dependent, but who can show that the son would, at a given period after enlistment, have contributed to her support;

OR Mothers who, as a result of change of financial circumstances, have subsequent to soldier son's enlistment become dependent or partly dependent will be treated from date of such change under the same conditions as wives when not in receipt of invalid, old age or war pension.

For invalid father who is a widower and is dependent upon the soldier for support—1/5 per diem.

For daughter of a soldier who is keeping house for her father who is a widower—1/5 per diem.

For soldier's sister who is a widow and who is solely dependent upon the soldier for support—1/5 per diem.

For brothers and sisters under the age of 16 years who are solely dependents upon the soldier for support—4½d. per diem.

For children, under 16 years of age, of a soldier's sister who is a widow and of whom the soldier is the sole support—4½d. per diem.

For children, under the age of 16 years, of a member of the A.I.F. who, after a Legal or Mutual Separation has been entered into, continues to maintain them by allotting portion of his military pay for such purposes—4½d. per diem.

EVERY MAN A VOLUNTEER

The exhortations and inducements used in Australia to persuade men to enlist were as old as the oldest society— the community's safety is at stake; your families are in peril; your religion is being derided, and so on. There was the added spur of mockery, overt or implied—a child asking, "What did you do in the War, Daddy?"; a strong-featured woman asking her man, "Will you go or must I?" By 1915 the art of poster propaganda was very well developed and worldwide, and outside the pornography of painted violence the themes were much the same whatever the nation. "Our" men were always firm-jawed and heroic, "Theirs" were fiercely evil and generally unshaven. The summarily pointing or beckoning finger was a universal symbol.

Perhaps it was because the battlefields of Europe were so distant, perhaps because the lure of England as "Home" was so strong that there entered into the early phase of recruitment in Australia an element of huckstering. It was as though a cheapjack travel agent was at work to persuade young men to seize their chance. The long casualty lists from the Dardanelles and the disasters of France and Flanders were yet to come; in the days before the end at Gallipoli, there was a fairground atmosphere about the urging to join for The Greatest Show on Earth.

To some extent it was true. It *was* exciting. The bands filling the streets with colour and cadence, the sense of swagger about the men already in uniform—all laid the groundwork for a widespread and very successful advertising campaign, certainly the best of its time. The campaign's theme was elemental and almost irresistible; the product offered free travel, excitement and a spice of danger and implied a just and rightful victory and the rewards that would follow. To ignore such a campaign could mean ostracism; to accept the challenge was to snatch at the chance of a lifetime.

Recruits march along a dusty road in northern New South Wales. Bandsmen often became stretcher bearers in action.

Infantrymen of the Australian Imperial Force march in a farewell parade along Collins Street, Melbourne, on September 25, 1914.
The day before war broke out, Australia offered Britain an expeditionary force of 20,000 men.

15

Schoolchildren in Hyde Park, Sydney, wave Union Jacks as the soldiers march by on their way to embark for service on Gallipoli.

WHAT WILL YOUR ANSWER BE

When your boy asks you—

"FATHER,—WHAT DID **YOU** DO TO HELP WHEN BRITAIN FOUGHT FOR FREEDOM IN 1915?"

ENLIST NOW

Families and well-wishers accompany volunteers bound for Gallipoli as they march down to the docks.

Troopships carrying the second contingent of the AIF lie at anchor in King George Sound, Western Australia.

ADVENTURE CRUISES

The assembly point for troopships from the Australian capital cities – and from New Zealand – was King George Sound in Western Australia. The first convoy left there on November 7, 1914, the second on December 31, taking the troops to Egypt for five months of intensive training before the decision was made to send them to Gallipoli.

Enlistment continued. Even after the initial wave of enthusiasm had subsided and emotional pressure had to be applied to entice men to join up, the excitement of what was still seen as an adventure cruise remained, and detachments of departing soldiers often made their farewells in rousing style.

MORE, AND STILL MORE MEN

KITCHENER'S MESSAGE

"The Australians and New Zealanders, combined with the Anglo-French forces in the Dardanelles, have already accomplished a feat of arms almost unexampled for its brilliance. To push the campaign to a successful conclusion, in each of the great Dominions new and large contingents are preparing.

The vital need is more and still more men.

The limitations of material have been surmounted and there are arms and clothing sufficient to convert all recruits into efficient soldiers. I took office as a soldier, not as a Politician; and I warned the country of the certainty that the war would be arduous and prolonged. I am of the same opinion now, and make an unrestricted call for men and a larger army. It is a matter for your conscience. Make up your minds quickly." KITCHENER.

The ferry Kulgoa conveys the first troops to leave Australia in World War I to the transport Berrima in Sydney Harbour. This force was sent to silence the German wireless stations and occupy German New Guinea.

JOIN TOGETHER
TRAIN TOGETHER
EMBARK TOGETHER
FIGHT TOGETHER

LIEUT. JACKA V.C

Enlist in the
Sportsmen's
Thousand

SHOW THE ENEMY WHAT
AUSTRALIAN SPORTING MEN CAN DO.

Top left: The Bushmen's Contingent leaves on the ship Euryalus. Groups such as bushmen and sportsmen were enlisted to fight as a team. Bottom: Troops embark on a passenger ship in Melbourne.

"A few of my mates and myself"

Australian soldiers enjoy a camel ride at the pyramids in Egypt. Many similar photographs were sent to families and friends.

Panorama of Mena Camp, in the desert near Cairo, where the Australian 1st Division underwent intensive war training.

Top left: Private Len Sawyer poses for a studio portrait in Cairo. Uniform, especially headgear, varied considerably; pith helmets were issued but were unpopular with the troops; the cane was a comic affectation. Above: Nurses of No. 3 Australian General Hospital form up to march into camp at Mudros on the island of Lemnos.

Heavily laden Australian soldiers pause for a photograph with a mounted Indian trooper near camp, probably on Lemnos. British and Empire troops assembled on Lemnos to prepare for the invasion of Gallipoli.

2

THE LAND
AND THE LANDING

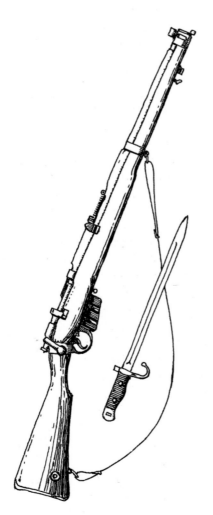

Short-magazine Mark IV Lee Enfield .303 rifle and 14-inch bayonet, standard issue for the British army up to World War II.

By March 1915 the decision had been made to mount a military assault on the Gallipoli peninsula. Chosen to make the attack in the north were the Anzacs, but they landed on the wrong beach. And the Turkish forces were there waiting for them.

Kitchener had begun to give serious consideration to a land battle as early as February. He was, after all, a fully professional soldier, and experience told him that if the Royal Navy did succeed in breaking through to Constantinople it would be essential to follow up quickly with a land force to exploit the success. His first thought was to send the British 29th Division of the regular army as far as the Greek island of Lemnos, about 65 kilometres from the entrance to the Dardanelles, but that plan was deferred when German successes against Russia meant the possible release of enemy divisions to fight elsewhere. It seemed sensible to keep the seasoned 29th at home for a while in case it was needed on the Western Front.

Much more conveniently situated was the Australian and New Zealand Army Corps, training under Birdwood in Egypt and expecting to fight in Europe. Churchill, convinced by March 23 of the need to strike by land, swung Kitchener to his way of thinking. Kitchener acted quickly, and by March 26 the troops in Egypt were given the order to stand by to sail for Lemnos. By that time they were already being called by the initial letters of their formal title. They were already known as Anzacs.

There was hardly an air of secrecy about the prospect of a military assault on the Dardanelles. On March 15 the French government actually issued an official note announcing the fact and stating that an expeditionary force under General Albert D'Amade was already in the Aegean. A week later – and without the benefit of a public announcement – the British and Empire troops were together in the fine harbour at Mudros on the island of Lemnos.

It was as well, perhaps, that there was no fanfare about that troop movement, for it would only have highlighted the fact that the first of the blunders which were to characterise the whole operation had already been made. With the navy's withdrawal after the battle of the 18th and the decision to attack by land, the movement of troops and matériel to Lemnos was begun hurriedly. It was not until all the ships were anchored there that it was discovered that in the rush the stowage of weapons, ammunition and supplies had been something of a haphazard affair and that ships' holds would have to be emptied and restowed. That could not be done in the open harbour at Mudros; the convoy would have to be sailed back to Egypt.

The men of the 3rd Australian Infantry Brigade watched the long line of ships sail away. In the plan prepared by Hamilton's staff it had been decided that if there was to be an assault they would be the first beach-storming party. They were left on Lemnos to spend more than a month practising landing operations.

Eighty kilometres across the water, the watching, waiting enemy made excellent use of the extra time, deepening and strengthening defences, stringing more wire, siting more machine-guns on fixed lines of fire. And the time was also well spent by the many Turkish and German agents in Egypt, who sent out a constant stream of information about Allied troop numbers and supplies.

German interest in Turkish military fortunes was no new development, nor something that stemmed merely from the war. The strategists in Berlin had been well aware of the Dardanelles, and German forces had been involved in Turkey ever since 1882, when Prussian officers, on request from the Sultan, were sent south in an attempt to modernise the Turkish army. The involvement continued in a loose fashion until, early in 1914, a more formal arrangement was made for both officers and NCOs of the regular German army to be attached to the Turkish forces and for all to be placed under the nominal command of a German naval officer, Admiral Guido von Usedom. Indeed, many of the operations departments of the Turkish government were run by Germans at that time, and a popular bon mot of the day in Constantinople and Berlin was "Deutschland über Allah."

The senior German soldier in Turkey was General Liman von Sanders, an astute professional who had been appointed in 1913 to lead a military mission to Turkey and to become Inspector-General of the Turkish army. By the outbreak of war, von Sanders had done much to restructure and train the poorly disciplined ranks, and there were German officers and NCOs stationed in every Turkish unit.

Von Sanders had done something else. In his first tours of inspection, he had been appalled at the weak and haphazard defences protecting the Dardanelles – and he was certain that in any war the strategic straits would invite attack. At his urging an entirely new defence plan was implemented, and by the outbreak of war it was well advanced. The naval assault of March 1915 served both to prove the value of von Sanders' training routine and defensive measures and to add conviction to the belief that a land attack was more than likely.

The German general's experienced eyes had marked four potential danger spots. To the east of the Dardanelles, on the high shoulder of Asiatic Turkey, there was open country, broad plains which were ideal for large-scale troop movements and a wide-sweeping outflanking of the coastal defences there. On the Gallipoli peninsula itself there was the narrowest part between the town of Gelibolu and the high ground at Bulair; a successful landing there could possibly cut the peninsula off like a dis- 23 eased appendix. Further south there were beaches where the Aegean washed ashore, and some of them offered fair toeholds. At the extreme southern end there were larger beaches still, and the toe of the peninsula could be fired upon and landed upon from three sides.

Under the shrewd and urgent guidance of General von Sanders, Turkish engineers and gunners rushed to complete and then improve defences in all those areas. And to man the new fortifications, von Sanders could draw on the vast resources of the still powerful Ottoman Empire. Some idea of the size of the Ottoman Empire at the outbreak of war can be gained by considering where its seven army corps headquarters were situated – at Constantinople, Adrianople, Salonika, Erzerum, Damascus, Baghdad and the Yemen, with independent commands based on Tripoli and the Hedjaz; these commands encompassed nearly 3 million square kilometres, or an area slightly larger than all of eastern Australia. At the time of the Gallipoli landings, the Turkish High Command – and that meant, effectively, the Germans – had close to 550 battalions of infantry available, almost 30,000 cavalrymen, more than 1,300 field guns and howitzers and 40 mountain batteries. All told, more than half a million men were immediately under arms, and something more than 100,000 of them, in solid and heavily armed positions, stood ready for the Allies at Gallipoli; as fate would have it, two-thirds of the Turks were concentrated within striking distance of the area that was to become known to the world as Anzac.

It was not until April 21 that the restowed convoy set out again for Lemnos, 150 ships carrying 120,000 men. Two days later they were anchored once more at Mudros with a commander who later recognised that "the landing of an army upon this theatre of operations involved difficulties for which no precedent was forthcoming in military history."

Hamilton and his staff had made an offshore reconnaissance of the peninsula early in April, steaming up and down the north-western shore to examine the terrain and the likely landing places. At Bulair, on the narrowest part of the peninsula, there were fortifications which had been built by British engineers during the Crimean War as protection against a Russian incursion, and what was known about those works was probably the most definitive information Hamilton had. That, and some scant and uncertain prior knowledge supplemented by the reconnaissance, showed Hamilton that there were three dominating features to consider. There was the Sari Bair range rising almost 300 metres in near perpendicular escarpments, a massive network of ravines and gullies, thick with scrubby and thorny growth. There was the plateau of Kilid Bahr, a natural fortification 200 metres high and heavily entrenched and gunned to cover the Narrows from attack. And there was Achi Baba, a 180-metre-high hill which dominated the southerly toe of the peninsula. A pleasant valley rose into the foot of the hill, and in the valley lay the village of Krithia. Around and between village and hill the Turks had dug and built a series of overlapping trench systems and strongpoints. From them, rifles and machine-guns could enfilade any forward movement; from behind, from Achi Baba itself, artillery positions had an unrestricted field of fire on the terrain below.

To go against these formidable natural obstacles, reinforced by prepared and determined forces, Hamilton had the 12,500 men of the experienced British 29th Division, which Kitchener had finally decided to release and which would land at Cape Helles in the south, a Royal Naval Division, an armoured car unit and a number of naval aircraft. Also under his command was a French Force of two infantry regiments of the Metropolitan Brigades, colonial infantry units of Senegalese and Zouaves, two cavalry regiments of Chasseurs d'Afrique and a battalion of the Foreign Legion – about 4,000 men in all. The main part of them were to make a diversionary landing across the straits at Kum Kale. And, under General Birdwood, there was the 1st Australian and New Zealand Army Corps, the Anzacs, some 35,000 strong. These

men, from every Australian state and from both islands of New Zealand, had, without exception, volunteered their services. It was part of the eager rush to come to the aid of "the Old Country", of "Mother England", of "Home" – that and the spur of excitement, the fast adrenalin flow which came from a mixture of the imagined romance and colour of war and ignorance of the distant outside world.

The ignorance was shared, in part, by the commanders of those men. They knew almost nothing about the place they were planning to attack. There had been Hamilton's sketchy offshore reconnaissance and, aside from that, only a little aerial observation by Royal Navy planes. But such was the lack of co-ordination or even friendly relations between army and navy that the pilots' and observers' reports were unknown to Hamilton's staff. Maps of the Gallipoli peninsula's interior were virtually non-existent, and the planners were, therefore, unable to let field commanders know anything

about roads or the availability of either shelter or water. The poet John Masefield, who served in the Red Cross and was on Lemnos during the Gallipoli campaign, wrote of that land that it had "a rough and steep coast, roadless, waterless, much broken with gullies, covered with scrub, sandy, loose and difficult to walk on and without more than two miles of accessible landing throughout its length. The trees are mostly stunted firs; on some hills there are small clumps of pine and the few water-courses are deep ravines showing no water. The hills are exceedingly steep, much broken and roughly indented with gullies, cliffs and narrow, irregular valleys."

Even if Hamilton and his staff had known how bad the terrain was, their estimates of the enemy they were to meet were only guesses or assumptions – the figures ranged upwards to more than 150,000 in the area, with something between 40,000 and 80,000 on the peninsula itself, 30,000 across the water of the Asian side 25 and more than 50,000 in reserve. Given any level of accuracy about those numbers and understanding that they represented well-dug-in, well-armed and prepared troops, it was obvious enough that the assault would not be easy. It was made harder for the Anzacs by a factor completely out of their hands – by maritime matters.

On Saturday, April 24, the men who were to make up the first wave of the assault force, two companies of each of the four battalions of the 3rd Australian Infantry Brigade – some 1,500 men – were taken aboard the battleships *Queen*, *Prince of Wales* and *London*. By three o'clock the next morning they were closing the coast and slowing in intense darkness. The troops were to go ashore in rowing boats, each group of three boats strung behind a steam launch. There were 12 sets of tows, and between 30 and 40 men could be packed into each boat, so that less than half the brigade which formed the spearhead of the assault would be put ashore in that first wave. They were the only men who stood any chance at all of reaching the land undetected, and however well trained they were, however eager for the battle, for the time between battleship and beach they were entirely in the hands of the Royal Navy.

Both the landing planning staff and the naval squadron responsible for putting the men ashore were commanded by Rear-Admiral C.F. Thursby. Under him, the most detailed plans were made to put the soldiers ashore at the right place and in good order. A crucial part of the plan was the placement of a marker to guide the assault boats inshore.

Stan Watson – later Lieutenant-Colonel Watson, CBE, DSO, MC, ED – was a young Signals officer on General Birdwood's staff at that time and privy to almost everything in which his commander was involved. Watson later recalled the events immediately preceding the landing, events that were to provoke controversy and debate in all the years after. According to Watson, the joint planning staff had originally arranged for a midget submarine to anchor close to the coast and shine a white

Top: As the sun rises over Chunuk Bair on April 25, 1915, strings of small boats carrying Anzac troops move from their transports towards Anzac Cove. Bottom: A boatload of British troops destined for the landing at Cape Helles passes HMS Implacable.

light seaward. This would enable the convoy to take up its correct position during the night and would also guide the flotilla of towed boats carrying the assault troops to the selected landing spot. For no apparent reason Admiral Thursby cancelled this arrangement; in place of the submarine close inshore, he ordered the battleship HMS *Triumph* to anchor seven kilometres out from the coast and shine its guiding light seaward from there. Watson maintained that the absence of a light close to the shore caused the ships' captains to misjudge their position when approaching the coast and resulted in the troops "being distributed along a mile of the wrong beach in the most haphazard disorder."

Watson's was only one of the explanations given for the faulty landing. The tide set was blamed, as was bad navigation and the darkness and any number of things. Hamilton himself later recalled, "A rugged and difficult part of the coast had been selected for the landing – so rugged that I considered the Turks were not at all likely to anticipate such a descent. Indeed, owing to the tows having failed to maintain their exact direction the actual point of disembarkation was rather more than a mile north of that

THE GENERAL THEY CALLED BIRDIE

So strongly has General William Birdwood become associated with the men he commanded at Gallipoli that it is often difficult to persuade Australians that he was an Englishman. Birdwood was, in fact, born of English parents in Poona, that most Blimpish-sounding Indian city, in 1865, and spent a privileged early childhood as the son of the Under-Secretary to the government of Bombay. As was common in those days for the sons of the ruling class in India, the lad was sent home to England for a proper education. And at 19, upon graduating from the Royal Military College at Sandhurst, Second Lieutenant Birdwood was posted to India, where he began a most illustrious career.

Virtually every officer on Indian service learned some local language or dialect. But Birdwood set out to know as much as he could about the country of his birth, and he became fluent not only in Hindustani but in Pushtu, Punjabi and Persian. He proved an excellent soldier as well; within six years he was promoted to captain, and shortly after the outbreak of the Boer War in 1899 he was appointed brigade major, a position in which he served as the executive officer to the brigadier commanding three regiments.

Every ambitious officer needs a mentor, and Major Birdwood found his in Lord Kitchener, Commander-in-Chief of Imperial forces in South Africa. Keen, disciplined and intelligent, Birdwood soon became Kitchener's military secretary and then went with him to India when Kitchener was named Viceroy in 1902. There followed a dazzling succession of assignments and promotions until, in 1915, the brilliant young Brigadier Birdwood was appointed to command the recently formed corps of soldiers from Australia and New Zealand. These were the troops destined to become enshrined in the pantheon of war as the Anzacs, and Birdwood would take his place among them.

The Anzacs were from the start a splendid body of men – every one a volunteer, almost universally in superb physical condition. Training his men in Egypt, Birdwood drove them hard, instilling discipline but also drawing out their natural resilience and self-reliance. He was not one of the headquarters generals; he was frequently among his men, and after the awful opening days at Gallipoli, they were quick to realise that he would fight and suffer with them. Major-General Birdwood was one of a number of senior officers whose names appeared on the casualty lists.

Like Kitchener, Birdwood had a shrewd eye for talented officers, and when it was finally decided to leave that agonising peninsula, it was Birdwood and his staff who ended an eight-month debacle with a safe and orderly withdrawal. For ever after, Birdwood and his Anzacs were inextricably joined by the bonds of battle.

In March 1916, scarcely three months after Gallipoli, Birdwood took the 1st and 2nd Australian divisions and the New Zealand Division to France, where the Anzac legend gained new dimensions in the blood-stained horror of the Hindenburg Line. There, under overall British command, the Australians were ordered to mount a daylight attack across open and difficult ground,

*Lieutenant-General
Sir William Birdwood*

with no artillery barrage to soften the enemy and cut his barbed wire. In two assaults on the German lines at Bullecourt in April and May 1917, Birdwood's Anzacs lost more than 10,000 killed and wounded – and lost, too, what little faith they had in the British High Command. But Birdwood was by then accepted as an Anzac.

In May 1918, after three years of leading the Anzacs in a succession of campaigns – including the horrific Passchendaele assault in which more than 25,000 Australians were killed, wounded or posted as missing in action – Birdwood handed over his Australian Imperial Force to his ablest subordinate, General John Monash. He himself was promoted to lieutenant-general and given command of the reconstituted British Fifth Army, holding the comparatively quiet southern sectors of the battlefield while his beloved Anzacs fought spectacularly well in the north.

Birdwood made two emotion-charged tours of Australia after the war, the first in 1920, the second in 1933, by which time he had served as Commander-in-Chief in India and had been elevated to field marshal. He was showered with honours, orders and decorations, passing up through a knighthood in the Order of St Michael and St George to be raised to the peerage in 1938. He died in 1951, at the age of 86. It is worth remembering that when he became a peer of the realm, the title he chose was Baron of Anzac and Totnes. To the Anzacs he honoured in taking that title he was always known simply as "Birdie."

which I had selected." Wherever the fault lay, the outcome of all the planning was that on a flat-calm sea and sheltered by a moonless night, the attack on Gallipoli began in the wrong place.

The men moving across the darkly calm water did not know that. They were jammed tightly together in the towed boats, wearing greatcoats, lumpy beneath the webbing straps which held their packs and ammunition pouches, bayonets, water-bottles and entrenching tools. Each man carried a spare water-bottle, 200 rounds of ammunition and two cotton bags slung to his waistbelt, each holding a day's rations of tea, sugar, bully beef and ship's biscuits, rough and hard as dog biscuits. Two empty sandbags were issued to every soldier going ashore so that individual protection could quickly become a parapet for a section of trench when a squad or platoon dug in. Bulky and laden, each of the men had to clamber down in the blackness into a bobbing boat, cramming himself in among his mates till the gunwales were close to the water, his rifle upright between his knees and his shoulders tight against the men on either side of him, their closeness at once a reassurance to themselves and a hindrance to the five sailors and the conning officer in each boat. The last vessel in each group of three was conned by a Royal Navy midshipman, a boy younger than the youngest soldier.

At 3.30 a.m. the boats began to move towards the barely seen bulk of the shore. Southwards, down at the tip of the peninsula, the ships carrying Britain's 29th Division were standing in towards the shore where there were to be appalling casualties in the storming of Cape Helles; across the straits the French and their Colonials and Legionnaires were aimed at Kum Kale; northwards, New Zealanders and men of the Royal Naval Division were moving in a feint against Bulair to keep the Turkish diverted from the main assault.

The grey part-light of false dawn showed a denser greyness where the shore loomed as the boats moved in. The men squinted to make out the features they had been shown on the map — 28 the bulk of Gaba Tepe, the spot called

Fisherman's Hut and the shelving beach between them. They had no idea of the strength of the northing current nor of Admiral Thursby's replacement of the inshore marker light, and when the first tentative shots came at them out of the still-black hills, they began to slip over the sides of the little boats into the water, making for a beach they had been told about. It was not there. They were beneath the rough hill of Ari Burnu; the Gaba Tepe beach was a kilometre and a half away on their right.

As the Australians moved in to where a thin, pale line of surf-wash marked the beach, those first suspicious shots became probing fire, the start of eight months of continuous shooting, and the first men had been struck. Sometimes the very closeness in the slow-moving boats stopped a man from toppling sideways after a bullet strike; sometimes a round would pass through a man and strike his neighbour also. Soldiers slipping over the sides of their boats found shingle below the waist-high water, found it sliding and carrying their feet from away from them. They had been told not to loop their epaulettes over the webbing straps of their equipment so that packs could be shed quickly if there was a need, but many of them, with steel-shod boots on that treacherous shingle, slid beneath the water before they could unburden themselves. The humped shapes of dead men

moved sluggishly in the wash of the surf, the blood in the water round them beginning to show pink as the sky lightened.

Behind them the pinnaces and their tows were swinging back towards the offshore fleet, where it was already becoming plain to the staff that the landing was not where it had been planned. It was too late to do anything about it, of course – the second wave was standing ready to go in, waiting to swing down into the little boats as soon as the dead and wounded had been lifted from them.

For the men ashore there was a mixture of bafflement and fear and a fierce determination. They knew the lie of the land was wrong and the features they hunted for were not there; but the enemy was, and that was enough to drive them up and off the bloody beach, uncertain of the way but sure of their abilities. They had no idea that they were creating a legend.

Fifteen years earlier, Australian troops in South Africa had shown their fighting qualities, a compound of adaptability, endurance, grim humour and, often enough, raw courage. The fact that many – perhaps most – of them enlisted to fight the Boers without any clear idea of the reasons for the fight did not diminish their worth as battlefield soldiers. Much the same lack of knowledge had brought a great many men

to Gallipoli. The reasons for joining in a distant war were hardly likely to be clear to Australia-at-large when they were unclear enough to the ordinary folk of Britain. Propaganda disguised as information brought a great swell of patriotic fervour, of support for the Motherland in Her Righteous War against the Forces of Evil, and drew men to the colours for reasons to do with emotion rather than logic or even common sense.

There was another similarity with that previous generation, the Boer War men. A considerable proportion of the soldiers wearing "Australia" on their uniforms were comparative newcomers to the country, emigrants from Britain. Some estimates have put the figure as high as 40 per cent, but whether it was that high or not it is certain that regional British accents were common in the Australian army in 1915. In view of that, it seems strange that virtually everyone writing of the Australians at that time appeared to see a different breed from the British norm. Masefield, for one, waxed lyrical, saying they were "the finest body of young men ever brought together in modern times. For physical beauty and nobility of bearing they surpassed any men I have ever seen; they walked and looked like the kings in old poems." Ellis Ashmead-Bartlett, representing the British press at Gallipoli, wrote, "This race of athletes 29

The Anzac Digger

proceeded to scale the cliffs without responding to the enemy's fire. They lost some men but did not worry."

Comments like those, written at the time often enough on the spot, paint a brave and beautiful picture. Photographs of the men themselves, at the time and on the spot, show as ordinary a selection of normal men as would be found anywhere, among them short ones, plump ones, callow-faced boys and middle-aged men, city lads and country fellows.Certainly they had the tan which the training time in Egypt had given them all, and they had the cockiness of a group well away from home and not deeply indoctrinated with a military discipline, but it seems improbable that they were anything radically different from or above an ordinary level.

And yet, there below the broken face of a cliff in a land most of them had never heard of a few weeks before, they began, together, to become something unique. They began to forge a steel-hard legend of something like invincibility as they fought their way off a narrow and blood-stained beach and moved in and up through a killing sweep of fire.

By nine that morning, the day was already building towards a sultry heat, and 8,000 men were ashore, moving ahead against the obstacles of wickedly rough country, map references which did not jibe with the actuality of the terrain and an enemy for whom there were plenty of targets. The Australians and New Zealanders, moving uphill all the time, were scattered by the broken country; they were soaked to the waist when they came off the beach and into the scrub, disoriented and with rifles clogged with damp sand. Officers soon found that their control of movement was ruined by the ground over which they fought to advance. A company going up to the attack, already reduced by the train of dead and wounded lying behind, would suddenly find a gully carving the land in the direction in which they were moving, splitting the company and widening the gap between its halves as the gully spread apart. Then the scarred cross-cuts in the land would further fragment the groups, and unity disappeared altogether. A concerted assault became a dozen minor actions, a platoon here, a section there, and always under the guns of the Turks, above them in solid trenches and off on the flank where field guns and mortars bombarded them from the height of Gaba Tepe.

Yet, with it all, it was still, at that stage, an advance. Despite their losses and despite the growing confusion on the narrow funnel of the crowded beach behind them, the troops were pushing forward and up and outward and were making ground. The most advanced groups of men found themselves all at once looking down on the blunt knoll of Ari Burnu and over the sweep of ugly country they had gained. But they had little time to exult. Strong fire struck at them from the far side of the plateau whose edge they had reached, and from the higher ridges beyond. That first day saw the establishment of a pattern of fire from above, a terrible pattern which did not vary from the beginning to the end of the Gallipoli campaign.

Behind those furthest advanced parties the flow of reinforcements continued, but in no smooth and concerted manner. Boats put in to several points, conned away from the near chaos of the beach, their courses changed because of Turkish shellfire, because of the hazard of broken boats lying half-submerged, because of the floating corpses and wreckage. Many boatloads of troops were put ashore against very steep cliffs and had to drag and claw themselves upwards under remorseless fire, their dead and wounded hanging suspended from thorn bushes or stunted trees or disappearing into the gullies which cracked the cliff-face apart. Yet through the bewilderment of the beach and up and over the nearby cliffs the movement forward did not stop.

Everything those men needed had to be brought with them, carried on their backs in the first instance, dumped ashore for their use after that and then manhandled forward. The land they had forced gave them nothing but discomfort and pain and death. There was no food or water, no shelter, no ammunition, no supplies

Johnny Turk

31

of any kind except what could be taken by physical effort from the water's edge and upwards. As the day and the fighting became hotter, the need for water was urgent. Carriers struggled up the craggy slopes with containers, often taking them up on the stretchers on which they would take down the wounded. And always under the punishing fire from above. Those stretcher-bearers – the troops called them "the Linseed Lancers" because they reputedly used linseed oil to patch up superficial wounds – and the doctors who worked grimly and bloodily with them were as much firing-line soldiers as any man with a rifle. They were as close to danger, and they died as suddenly.

There was no front line, no continuous stretch of country that could be construed as a front. Men came ashore as best they could and moved as fast as they could to get under cover. In that haste, units were broken and groups of men were seized by officers and put to the fight with strangers as often as not, piecemeal and puzzled. The scattered landings, the wrong beach and the non-stop fire made precise orders and manoeuvres impossible; the assault became largely a matter of individual initiatives, often of junior officers and NCOs making fast decisions for small parties of rapidly tiring men.

The first inland ridge had been taken early in the day – and one group of Australians on the edge of exhaustion had scaled the odd upthrust of rock which became known as the Sphinx, virtually dragging themselves to the top. Just the fact that they had reached the top was enough to send the Turkish soldiers there down on the far side, and that meant some easing of the fire on the men below, the ones heading across the rough floor of a narrow valley towards the second ridge. One very small party struggled onto the high flank of the third ridge; from there they could see away down to where the waters of the Narrows shone in the sunlight, an objective never to be reached and, when that party was forced back for lack of reinforcement, an objective not seen again during the campaign.

By the middle of the day the gullies of the second ridge, the ragged slopes of the rise known as Baby 700 (it sat on the 700-foot contour line) and the narrow finger of land leading to it and called the Nek were all a killing ground for Turks, Australians and the New Zealanders now inextricably mixed with them. Baby 700 was to change hands five times that day.

An indication of the difficulties the invaders faced, of the extraordinary toughness of the terrain, is that the 12,000 troops ashore by mid-afternoon were faced by a local defensive force of only 4,000 Turks – and could not break through them. The Anzacs were spread piecemeal across an arc of immensely difficult country; they moved forward and up whenever they could, but seldom in solidly linked groups, for the cut of the country tended to isolate them from one another. So uncoordinated and scattered were the troops and so difficult was it to take fixed positions from below that Turks who had been outflanked and bypassed actually found themselves able to fire on the Anzacs from behind. Indeed, fire struck into every part of the invading force. There was no position anywhere between the furthest inland probe and the beach three kilometres behind which was not in range of Turkish gunfire, and men died as fast at the edge of the sea as they did on the jagged hills beyond.

There was a third and crucial factor against the Anzacs on that day to add to the five-week delay caused by the faulty ship loading and the catastrophe of being landed on the wrong beach. That extra factor was a 35-year-old Turkish general called Mustafa Kemal – intelligent, quick on his feet and very professional. Kemal was commander of the division in reserve near the Narrows and had his best regiment on field manoeuvres when news of the landing reached him. This regiment was in the firing line less than three hours later, and by then Kemal was organising the rest of his division to move forward. Faced with those fresh and first-class troops under skilled command, the Anzacs had no hope of breaking the Turks that day.

By late afternoon the sky had clouded over and the flat heat became dull and oppressive. The forward troops were almost without water and close to collapse. Baby 700 was yielded to the Turks finally, a rise of land surrounded and covered by the dead of both sides. The New Zealanders hung on to the edge of the Nek for as long as they could before giving up that grisly promontory. Their withdrawal was part of a general pull-back in the face of the renewed ferocity Kemal's men had put into the battle.

By early evening the clouds seemed to touch the ground, and they wept a thin and soaking drizzle on the exhausted men. Field commanders watching their troops staggering down the rocky tracks to places of marginal shelter assessed their fighting capacity as very low. The guns of the Indian Mountain Battery which had been dragged up into precarious firing positions had been abandoned when the Turks launched a savage attack against them. The beach was a crowded shambles, so littered with lines of wounded that it was difficult to pick a way to the sea. Units were scattered and fragmented, and communication was difficult.

Birdwood had spent the day aboard ship off shore, assessing as best he could the messages and signals sent out to him. Much of what filtered through came, unfortunately, from wounded men brought off the beach and was undoubtedly less than accurate. It was not until late in the evening, when his two divisional commanders, Australia's General William Throsby Bridges and New Zealand's General A.J. Godley, asked him to come ashore that Birdwood was able to hear their direct and informed opinions and make his own assessment. Given that both generals were suggesting — almost insisting on — withdrawal, Birdwood reluctantly dictated a message to Hamilton aboard the flagship, *Queen Elizabeth*. It said, in part, "The men are thoroughly demoralised by shrapnel-fire to which they have been subjected all day after exhaustion and gallant work in the morning. If troops are subjected to shell fire again tomorrow morning there is likely to be a fiasco."

By the time Hamilton replied that re-embarkation was impracticable, Birdwood — not anxious to withdraw in the first place — had reconsidered. His commander's signal to him included the injunction to "make a personal appeal to your men and Godley's to make a supreme effort to hold their ground. You have got through the difficult business, now you have only to dig, dig, dig, until you are safe."

When Birdwood got that message it was fully dark and stormy; the rain by now was heavy and the seas were running high enough to have made a withdrawal in small boats and under fire a near impossibility. Those same conditions wiped out any chance of reinforcements coming ashore under cover of darkness. The downpour washed over the dead and the wounded still lying out on the high ground. Narrow gullies which had been dust-dry that morning ran with bloody water, and the bone-weary, soaking men huddled where they could away from the driving rain and the incessant fire.

The furthest point held that night in the broken crescent of positions was less than 2,000 metres from where the boats had deposited the first wave of men at dawn. Each side had lost about 2,000 dead, but the Anzacs had suffered the more serious loss of surprise. The enemy knew where they were, knew they could be held, knew they could be driven back.

Without the breakout on that first day, it was always probable that the campaign would be lost. The enemy had known for weeks that they were coming and had prepared well; the tiny beach the Anzacs had struck was not then and never would be an adequate bridgehead. They had had the ill-luck to encounter the crack troops of Mustafa Kemal and that officer's drive and military brilliance. The urgency of the assault and the impetus of the thrust inland were gone, and it was now to become a matter of clinging grimly to whatever dangerous footholds had been gained. Hamilton had given the word to "dig, dig, dig" — and Gallipoli, for the Anzacs, was already becoming another kind of trench warfare as darkness covered the exhausted troops, their wounded and their dead on that 25th of April, the first Anzac Day.

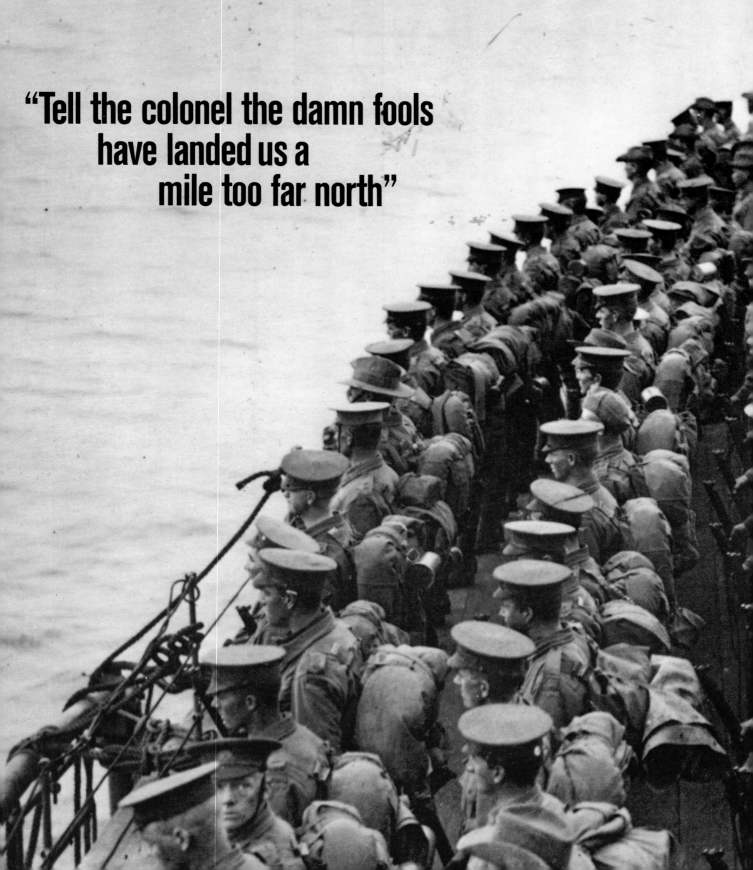

"Tell the colonel the damn fools have landed us a mile too far north"

THE INVASION BEGINS

Despite the confusion of the Gallipoli landing and the bloody fighting that followed, a number of men found time to record their impressions of the events in which they were taking part. Private Leslie Lott, a former carpenter from Sydney, was one of them. He had been among those left on Lemnos while the invasion convoy had steamed back to Egypt to unload and restow its cargo. "We put in nearly three weeks on the island doing some severe training," he noted. "In the mornings we went ashore practising landing, jumping into the water and rushing different hills. . . . In the afternoons we had lectures on what we were going to do when we landed on Turkish soil. . . . We were to carry 3 days rations and a full water bottle. We were to capture Maidos in that time. We thought we would get to Constantinople within a month."

The reality was somewhat different from what they were led to expect, partly owing to the fact that the first wave of the assault force landed in the wrong place. Commander C.C. Dix, the Senior Naval Officer in charge, commented: "Some of us were aware that we were some way north of our objective. . . . 'Tows steer more to starboard,' was ordered – only two crews complied. Twelve tows finished up in a cluster around Ari Burnu. I then shouted, 'Tell the Colonel the damn fools have landed us a mile too far north.' "

Out in the convoy, Australia's official war correspondent, C.E.W. Bean, was recording his impressions. At 4:38 a.m. he noted: "Listening eagerly, I catch faintly on a gust off the shore a distant knocking, as if someone had held up a small wooden box and knocked the inside out of it. It comes again and again continuously like the knock-knocking of an axle box heard very far off, very faint, through the bush. There is no mistaking it; though it is the first time I have heard the sound – it is the distant echo of rifle firing. " Australia's baptism of fire had begun.

HMS London, with troops of the 11th Battalion assembled on the forecastle, steams behind HMS Bacchante en route from Lemnos to Gallipoli.

A string of small boats loaded with New Zealand troops sets out for Anzac Cove in one of the follow-up waves.

Soldiers clamber down a rope ladder into a small boat waiting to be towed ashore. This photograph and the one overleaf were published in the Sydney Mail on July 7, 1915; since communications were slow and military censorship was very tight, newspapers used these pictures taken during training to bring a sense of immediacy to their story.

"In their eagerness to charge the Turks," the Sydney Mail commented, *"some of the Australians leaped into the water before the boats reached the beach.*

GETTING A TOEHOLD

While Anzac forward troops began pushing inland and up toward the first ridge, behind them began the build-up at Anzac Cove as the second and third waves were landed. Leslie Lott, who was in one of the follow-up waves, noted: "We climb over the side into small boats, and shells are splashing all around us. We reach the shore and dash across the beach. The artillery and machine-gun fire is hot and many never reach dry land. We made straight up the gully, working uphill all the time, the bullets and shrapnel pellets buzzing about like bees and tearing up the dust. It is hard to say how many went under. All the time snipers are at work and the shrapnel falling like hail and gradually thinning our ranks."

Troops continued to land throughout the day. During the morning the divisional headquarters staff came ashore; among them was C.E.W. Bean, who immediately began to take photographs of the men landing.

Divisional headquarters staff wade ashore at Anzac Cove. Everyone from batman to brigadier carried his own equipment and rations.

Headquarters of the Australian 1st Division disembark from small boats during a lull in the Turkish bombardment.

One of the horses landed on Gallipoli swings high in a sling coming off the ship. There was little use for horses at Anzac;
the Light Horsemen who served on Gallipoli left their mounts in Egypt.

Men pass supplies from hand to hand along one of the piers to the throng of soldiers on the narrow strip of beach.

Infantrymen move up under heavy packs towards Plugge's Plateau. Soldiers had to carry clothing, rations, blankets, a filled waterbottle and entrenching tools as well as a rifle and ammunition.

A team of soldiers strain forward to manhandle a heavy field gun up a track and into position.

Above: Troops gather at the first Ordnance Depot established near the southern end of Anzac Cove on April 26, after forward troops moved on. Right: Private J.B. Bryant holds an enemy shell case in an abandoned Turkish trench. The second day of fighting saw the 8th Infantry Battalion holding what had been a Turkish position along Bolton's Ridge.

"I do not order you to attack, I order you to die"

JOHNNY TURK

During the 13th century, a central Asian tribe known as the Ottomans settled in Asia Minor. By the 15th century they had conquered Byzantium and in time controlled a huge sweep of the world stretching from the Russo-Polish borders into north Africa. This vast Ottoman Empire had declined by the time of World War I, but whatever material losses 20th century Turkey had sustained, there remained, unchanged, two intangibles – the warrior inheritance and the disciplined faith of Islam.

With those things in his armoury, "Mehmetchik", the "Johnny Turk" who faced the Anzacs, was a formidable foe. His clothing and equipment were poor by Western standards and his education was at a generally low level, but he was fighting for his faith and country and he did it with a dogged courage in defence and a suicidal attacking flair which made him fearsome in a frontal assault, though he took dreadful casualties. Very few Turkish soldiers deserted, but they drew on a common faith to send messages to the many Moslem Indians opposing them, trying to persuade them to turn on their Christian officers.

The Turkish soldier's officers and senior NCOs had the twin benefits of some very solid German training and the tough combat experience of the Balkan Wars; led by them, Johnny Turk was a brave and difficult enemy with a strong sense of humour and a humanity that often surprised the Anzacs. He also had an obvious respect for his opposite number, as the metal cigarette case which was lobbed into Quinn's Post in November showed; it was awkwardly inscribed in bad French, " Take, with pleasure. To our heroic enemy." It was part of the odd friendship that sprang up between the men of the two sides, a battlefield friendship born of suffering the same deprivations and dangers and drawing together men who shared the rare virtue of enduring courage.

Turkish troops of the 25th Infantry Division get ready to move to the front. As often happened, they were addressed by their commanding officer and by a government official.

1. Sultan of Turkey   2. Enver Pasha, Turkish War Minister, whose attempt to "dig-out this hornet's nest" of Australians dismally failed
3. The German Kaiser's favourite portrait of himself   4. General Liman von Sanders   5. General von der Goltz

ENEMY ARCH-CONSPIRATORS AND THEIR CHIEF LIEUTENANTS AT THE DARDANELLES

FATHER OF THE TURKS

The man the Anzacs faced at Gallipoli was known then as Mustafa Kemal. He had been born into a poor family in Salonika late in 1880 and named Mustafa; the other part, Kemal, was a nickname meaning "perfection". He was a good student and did well at the military academy he attended, although he made few friends. Even as a youngster he had a certain grimness about him, an introverted air which kept people a little at bay.

Mustafa was one of the early members of the Young Turk movement and a willing worker for — and then Chief-of-Staff to — Enver Pasha, the colourful and dashing front-runner in that revolution which demanded a constitutional government for Turkey. Following their rising in 1908, they forced the last Sultan to yield to their demands and eventually give up his throne. Enver became the country's leader and, with Mustafa as his principal military planner, took the Turkish Empire into war in Libya and in the Balkans and then, on the side of Germany and Austria-Hungary, into World War I.

By then Mustafa Kemal, who had fallen out more than once with Enver over both military and political matters, was a lieutenant-colonel commanding a division of troops near Maidos, on the Gallipoli peninsula. His actions in the Dardanelles as a soldier of determination, bravery and brilliance gave him great standing among soldiers. News of his successes against the Allies spread through the civilian population so that he was acclaimed as "The Saviour of Gallipoli." Certainly his values were recognised by the men of influence in Turkey after World War I, and despite his discomforting manner, his icy blue eyes and frequent rages, he was seen as a man of promise and as a leader.

This man of military genius soon showed himself as a master of the political scene. After calling a national congress, he was elected president of a provisional national government early in 1920. From then until his death in 1938 he was never out of control in Turkey, and he saw the country through its establishment as a recognised and modern state, abolishing the harem, the veil and the fez, giving Turkish women their freedom and outlawing polygamy. He introduced the Roman alphabet, the Gregorian calendar, the metric system and a Western legal system as well as a host of other major reforms. Under Mustafa Kemal's presidential dictatorship, Turkey was the first Islamic nation to separate Church and State. And when in 1934 he decreed that every Turk had to register a surname, Mustafa Kemal received the surname Atatürk — "Father of the Turks."

Mustafa Kemal holds a roadside briefing on his defence perimeter. The staff car, supplied by the German army, allowed Kemal to maintain mobile control of his sector.

A camouflaged Turkish field kitchen on Gallipoli.

The Turkish corps commander, Essad Pasha (seated), holds a conference with his staff on a hill overlooking the battleground.

Officers and men of the Turkish 125th Regiment wait in one of their trenches. The depth and solidity of their positions contrasted sharply with the much weaker trench systems of the Anzacs.

An Allied soldier gives a wounded Turk a drink. Prisoners, though few, were well treated by both sides.

A party of Turkish prisoners line up for work.

RESPECTED ENEMIES

"I do not order you to attack," Mustafa Kemal told his troops, "I order you to die." And die they did, in fearful numbers. After one suicidal attack, a captured Turkish soldier told his Anzac captors: "I tried to return to my comrades and was fired on by both sides. I got to about ten yards of your trenches and crawled among the heaps of dead and pretended to be dead also. When it was daylight I saw one of your men looking at me through a periscope and heard someone calling in Turkish, 'Anyone alive there?' Then someone threw a stone and I realised they knew I was not dead and I answered, 'I am afraid of you and I cannot walk.' Then someone threw me a rope which I caught and was pulled in. Thanks be to God that I am with you in safety. We have to fight, as it is a Jehad, but we long for peace."

Turkish dead lie in no man's land after their disastrous attack on Australian positions on May 19. The subsequent armistice to bury the dead began a change of attitudes between Turks and Anzacs.

Bomb craters and ruined buildings reveal the extent of the British naval bombardment of Chanak, on the eastern side of the Dardanelles.

Turkish soldiers who opposed the Anzac landing are decorated for their bravery during the Gallipoli campaign.

Mustafa Kemal visits graves of men of the 5th Turkish Brigade. In 1934, speaking at a ceremony for the Anzac dead, Kemal – then Atatürk – said, "Having lost their lives on this land, they have become our sons as well."

3

LIVING HARD, DYING HARD

With a precarious toehold gained at Anzac Cove, it was a matter of digging in and holding on while under constant enemy fire. Casualties were high on both sides, and after the battle of May 19 an armistice was arranged to bury the reeking dead.

In the first week of the campaign, as April slid away, the Anzacs' casualties totalled more than 6,500, a quarter of them dead. The Turks suffered even more heavily, for although there had been less than 1,000 of them in the immediate area of the landing – strengthened very quickly by a further 3,000 – more and more reinforcements were rushed forward. Mustafa Kemal, incisive and determined to throw the infidel invaders back into the sea, launched attack after attack in brutally simple frontal moves. Yet despite the Turkish losses, the replacements came quickly and then were just as quickly strengthened, so that there was soon a near balance of numbers between attackers and defenders. And even now, as a bloody stalemate began to develop, the area held by the Anzacs had developed a sort of settled and familiar character – place-names bestowed, tracks worn and, somehow, the whole dreadful circumstance dealt with as a usual lifestyle.

Birdwood's 35,000 men had been reinforced by three battalions of Royal Marines, a mixed bag which included a considerable number of youngsters barely out of recruit training. But the arrival of these 1,800 additional men at least gave Birdwood the chance to reorganise his

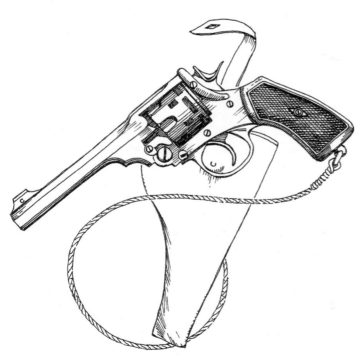

Mark VI Webley .45 revolver, the British service pistol introduced in 1915 and still used in World War II.

troops and to fill some of the fearsome gaps the fighting had made. The principal line of positions ran roughly parallel to the coast, reaching up along Bolton's Ridge through Lone Pine and on to the three posts – Steele's, Courtney's and Quinn's. There was a gap then, the savagely broken terrain across Bloody Angle and Dead Man's Ridge to Pope's Hill and then to the transverse line of Walkers Ridge with the length of Russell's Top leading to it. Shrapnel Gully and Monash Valley led up from Anzac Cove to Pope's Hill and then, beyond, off the edge of Walker's Ridge, there was the death trap of the Nek below Baby 700 and Mortar Ridge. The entire line was barely 3,000 metres long and only a little more than 1,000 metres at its furthest from the coast – and all of it, except a few reverse slopes, was under observation and under fire. Nonetheless, ammunition and supplies and replacements were coming ashore regularly; the beach became a mounting stockpile. The Turkish attacks were held and hurled back with awful losses, and Birdwood launched a major attack of his own during the night of May 2, sending troops in to take the Nek and Baby 700.

It was a disaster, badly timed and badly co-ordinated, and it cost 1,000 men dead, another 1,000 wounded and the utter exhaustion of the entire assault force. It was to be the last staged attack of any size for some time. Hamilton ordered that the emphasis at Anzac should be on standing fast and keeping as many Turks as possible tied down so that they could not be released against the Cape Helles forces. So for the first half of May it was a question of digging in further, of learning to master a few essential survival techniques, of coping.

During that time, four battalions of New Zealanders and the 2nd Australian Infantry Brigade were moved south, down to Cape Helles to reinforce the French-supported British attack there. Since their desperately costly landing on April 25, the British had been held and held again, and their first objective remained untaken.

Less than two months earlier, on March 18,

when the naval battle was raging, a party of British marines had landed unopposed near Sedd el Bahr at the toe of the peninsula. They had walked north through the village of Krithia, where they had bought fruit from the Turkish villagers, and then had gone on to scramble up the towering hill which rose north and east of Krithia. The hill was Achi Baba, and it was the first major objective of the British attack. On March 18th it had been undefended and could have been taken and held by a battalion.

The crack 29th Division and the French had already gone against Krithia once in a fruitless attempt to break through to that vital height. In that First Battle of Krithia, the Allied assault force totalled 14,000, and 3,000 of them were killed or wounded. They were to try again, this time with Anzacs added to their strength. The second assault was no more imaginative, no less clumsy than the first – poor intelligence, inadequate briefings, a haphazard preliminary bombardment and a frontal advance. The battle lasted three days, and that any headway was made at all is greatly to the credit of the Anzacs. The New Zealanders fought tigerishly, put to the attack again and again, uphill and in the face of a murderous fire, much of it from machine-guns in well-dug-in positions. Although they could not break that line, they demoralised the Turks by their fierce courage.

The Australians were no more successful in breaking through, but also provided a mass display of determined bravery, charging up out of their positions and forward to the Turks in a great waving line. It was as gloriously courageous an episode as any in the history of warfare, and totally futile. The Anzacs at the Second Battle of Krithia lost a third of their men for no material advantage: the New Zealanders lost just under 800 men out of the 2,600 who began the assault, the Australians went in 2,900 strong and lost 1,056. Those losses were all killed or wounded; there were no Anzac prisoners taken at the Second Battle of Krithia. The survivors were sent back up into the cauldron further north, and the Turks held the village and the dominating height of Achi Baba, 59 where the Royal Marines had munched their fruit a few weeks earlier.

At Anzac Cove and in the arc of positions round it, there was no hour without casualties in that first half of May, no time of day or night when the stretcher-bearers were not lurching and stumbling down the rocky tracks with their bloody burdens. It was in that time that one of these stretcher-bearers, Private Simpson, entered legend by commandeering a donkey and, without orders, began a ritual of moving the men down to the doctors at the beach, until he and his donkey were finally killed on May 19.

The troops were isolated, and they knew it. On the Western Front the fighting men had the knowledge that behind the lines, within reach, there were places set aside for rest. On Gallipoli there were no such havens. The sea was behind them, home was half a world away and the front was everywhere; the only way out was through the shock and pain of a wound. Tension was a constant, for there was almost no place in which a man could stand and relax, nowhere his body could not be reached and ruptured by shrapnel or bullet. In the trenches and forward posts where men scratched down into the land for shelter, the simple accident of standing upright could bring instant death from a Turkish sniper's bullet or an air-burst.

There was, too, a feeling about the Turk which was a part of the general lack of knowledge about the war and its reasons. There had been enough propaganda to leave some simple statements in many minds as truth: the Turk was not "a white man", not a Christian; he was "a native" an old-time heathen, fighting under the banner of Allah, and any atrocities could be believed of him. In the almost mindless butchery of the first day on Gallipoli and in the savagery of the days that followed, stories spread — that the Turk mutilated the wounded, tortured and killed prisoners, castrated captives and left them to bleed to death.

On the Turkish side there was the feeling of violation, of the invasion of the homeland by unbelievers. The soldiers were told by Mustafa Kemal: "To carry out the honourable duty entrusted to us there must not be one step towards the rear. All our comrades agree that they will show no signs of fatigue until the enemy are finally hurled into the sea."

There was, then, a mixture of bigotry and fanaticism at work from either side and a consequent ferocity in the incessant fighting through till mid-May. By then the Anzacs had adapted remarkably well to the conditions, had gained a swift understanding of the terrain and the way to move and fight in it. And whatever the beliefs were about the Turk as a barbarous heathen, they waned gradually and died once and for all in the week that began on May 19.

Early that morning, the Turks threw a mas-

Simpson (left) and Henderson in action with their donkeys.

THE DONKEY MEN

Simpson and his donkey are part of the legend of Anzac, and yet, like very many of the men in Australian uniform, Simpson was an Englishman. Born John Simpson Kirkpatrick in the northern county of Durham, he was just 21 at the outbreak of war, but by then he had already been to sea as a stoker, had jumped ship in Australia and become a miner in Queensland and then gone back to sea again. He enlisted under his middle name for some reason and became an ambulance-man and stretcher-bearer in the Medical Corps. Like the other men of the force that sailed from Australia, he expected to go to England, and he hoped to see his family again before being sent on to the battlefields of France. Instead

sive attack against the Anzac positions. There had been dispute about the main thrust of that attack; Kemal and his fellow divisional commander, Essad Pasha, had planned a single and concentrated spearpoint assault at the Nek and into Monash Valley; Liman von Sanders argued for an attack along the entire length of the line. He got his way and lost the battle. On May 11 Birdwood had written to Lord Kitchener, "My men are A1 in attack but curiously callow and negligent, and the only thing I fear is a really heavy night attack driven home against one part of my line, as I cannot get the men to bestir themselves and hurry up to repulse an attack at once." Thanks to von Sanders' decision, Birdwood had no reason to fear.

There was a first warning when Turkish gunfire slackened and fell away into a near silence. It was a little after 3 a.m. The sky was exceptionally clear and bright, and some of that brightness caught the thousands of bayonets as the great mass of Turkish troops was readied for the assault. Below the higher ground between Lone Pine and German Officer's Ridge, the Turks had moved their 2nd, 5th and 16th divisions, almost 40,000 troops.

In the alertness brought on by the suddenly reduced barrage, the steel reflections of the Turkish bayonets were enough warning. The Anzacs opened fire at once, and the desperate Turks were then forced to go forward into that fire, to follow a plan that had already miscarried. For them it was as grievous an error and as bitter a blood-letting as the Anzac landing had been less than a month earlier. For the Anzacs it was a little like an old-fashioned European battle, Australians and New Zealanders rising in their positions and aiming volley fire into the close-packed ranks of a fully expected and completely exposed advance. They could not miss their targets, and as long as they stood firm they could not lose that day. The Turks pushed their attack hard, but there was no way they could drive it home in the face of that concentrated and remorseless fire hitting them while they were massed in open ground. A handful of them managed to get past some outlying positions only to find themselves enfiladed from both flanks and their rear by New Zealanders who cut them down to a man.

About 13,000 Anzacs held the line that day against almost three times their number. When the Turks withdrew, routed, they left behind 10,000 casualties, more than 3,000 of them killed. Ahead of the Anzac posts the devastated landscape was heaped and piled with dead and dying men, and the growing heat of the day brought the evil smell of corrupting flesh. The monstrous hum of the swarms of flies almost obliterated the moans of the wounded.

By afternoon the stench had become almost unbearable. Although some shots were still

there was Egypt and then Gallipoli.

The legend of Simpson began to build on the very first night ashore. The *Official History* reports, "On the night of April 25 he annexed a donkey, and each day and half of every night, he worked continuously between the head of Monash Valley and the beach. Simpson escaped death so many times that he was completely fatalistic; the deadly sniping down the valley and the most furious shrapnel fire never stopped him." It became a familiar grouping—the little, gentle-faced donkey, a bloodied figure slumped on its back and the solid shape of the soldier alongside, an arm around the wounded man. No one kept count of how many men Simpson saved, but they numbered in the hundreds. His commanding officer, seeing what good work Simpson was doing, let him get on with it as long as he reported at his ambulance unit once each day.

The last report Simpson made was when he and his donkey, which he had named Murphy, called at the unit on May 19. Later that day he was moving back along a creek bed, a wounded man leaning on his shoulder and another on Murphy's back. A shell burst close above them on the lip of the creek. Both the men were wounded again, and Simpson was killed instantly by a piece of shrapnel in the heart. He was 23 and a piece of Australian history.

Simpson had a counterpart among the New Zealanders. Lieutenant James Henderson came from a tiny place called Kihikihi on the North Island. He and his brother Jack enlisted with the Auckland Mounted Rifles, a regiment which, like the Light Horsemen of Australia, fought at Gallipoli as infantry, and James also acquired a donkey and a reputation for unshaken bravery under fire.

Like Simpson, he took to moving wounded men to the comparative safety of the dressing stations behind the trenches, but he lived a little longer than Simpson. On August 9, men of his regiment were sent to reinforce the Wellington Battalion in assault. Of the 248 Aucklanders who went into the attack, only 52 came out, almost all of them wounded, including Henderson's brother Jack. Henderson was not among them; he was killed that night and, like Simpson, still lies in a Dardanelles grave.

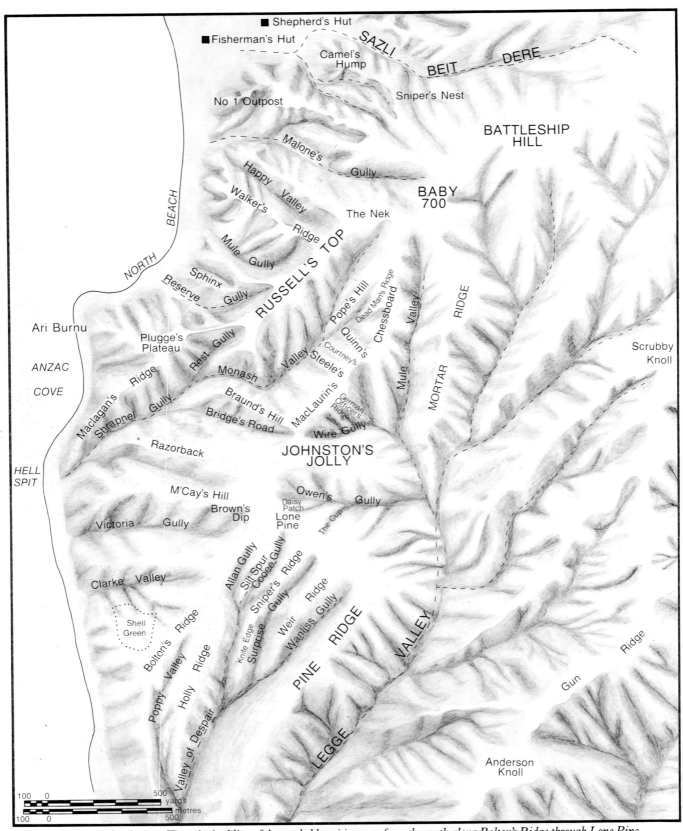

■ Shepherd's Hut

■ Fisherman's Hut

SAZLI

BEIT   DERE

Camel's
Hump

Sniper's Nest

No 1 Outpost

BATTLESHIP
HILL

Malone's

Gully

BABY
700

Happy   Valley

Walker's

The Nek

NORTH   BEACH

Ridge

RUSSELL'S   TOP

Mule   Gully

Sphinx

Reserve   Gully

Pope's Hill

Dead Man's Ridge

Chessboard

Mule   Valley

MORTAR   RIDGE

Ari Burnu

Plugge's
Plateau

Rest   Gully

Quinn's

Courtney's

Scrubby
Knoll

ANZAC

COVE

Maclagan's   Ridge

Monash

Valley

Steele's

Braund's Hill

MacLaurin's   Ridge

German
Officer's
Ridge

Shrapnel   Gully

Bridge's Road

Wire   Gully

HELL
SPIT

Razorback

JOHNSTON'S
JOLLY

M'Cay's Hill

Brown's
Dip

Owen's   Gully

Daisy
Patch

Lone
Pine

The Cup

Victoria   Gully

Allan Gully

Silt Spur

Cooee Gully

Sniper's   Ridge

Clarke   Valley

Knife Edge

Surprise   Gully

Weir   Ridge

Wanliss Gully

PINE   RIDGE

VALLEY

Shell
Green

Bolton's   Ridge

Holly   Ridge

Poppy   Valley

Gun   Ridge

LEGGE

Valley of Despair

Anderson
Knoll

100   0   500
                       yards
                       metres
100   0   500

The Anzac battle area. The principal line of Anzac-held positions ran from the south along Bolton's Ridge through Lone Pine to Steele's, Courtney's and Quinn's posts.

being exchanged, both Red Cross and Red Crescent flags were raised and stretcher-bearers ran hesitantly from both sides to collect the wounded. That move was unofficial, prompted by mutual horror and disgust, but it led to formal approaches being made for a nine-hour armistice on May 24. By that time most of the wounded were dead.

One edge of the arena was a field of standing corn with the butterfly colours of poppies mixed into it. The corn and the adjoining scrub had been cut, reaped into swathes where the intensity of the gunfire had harvested plants and men together. Gullies of scrub-oak and myrtle were part-filled with bodies which had crushed the foliage, and the stink of death mixed with the scent of the aromatic leaves. There were shell craters which had become mass graves and windrows of Turks lying in stacked lines where the fire had taken them.

During the armistice, the Anzacs gained a new perspective on the Turks as men from the opposed sides mingled, searching for wounded among the piled bodies. Anzacs knelt to hold water-bottles to the lips of parched Turkish wounded, passed cigarettes, exchanged small souvenirs with these enemy soldiers and found that they were not barbarous savages but men like themselves. They were a little smaller perhaps, a different shade, and they spoke a different tongue, but they were plainly soldiers, dirty, exhausted, miserable at the work they were doing and capable of friendly and humane gestures. While the man in the trench opposite might still be the enemy, he was never again the fiend the propagandists had suggested him to be. Indeed, an odd sort of camaraderie sprang up with "Johnny Turk", a recognition of his human and soldierly qualities and of the fact that he was undergoing the same sort of privation as his enemies.

And then the brief armistice was over. The human face of the enemy had been seen; but when the flags of truce went down, the gunfire began again at once.

In sharp contrast to the battlefields of Europe, Gallipoli presented as much immediate danger

Top: Captain Sam Butler leads the blindfolded Turkish envoy, Major Kemal Ohri, out of Anzac Cove after arranging an armistice to bury the dead following the massacre of May 19. Bottom: Soldiers recover and bury the rotting bodies of their dead comrades during the nine-hour truce on May 24. Some of the saps between opposing trenches were used as mass graves.

to senior officers as to troopers. Birdwood himself was barely spared by a Turkish bullet which grazed his scalp; although the wound became septic, it cleared up in a week and had no effect on his efficiency. General Bridges was less lucky. On May 15 he was on his way through Monash Valley, where Turkish snipers were inflicting constant casualties. The general's party ran from cover to scant cover and reached a dressing-station below Steele's Post, where Bridges stopped long enough for a brief talk and a cigarette with the men there. Then he ducked around the next traverse, and the men following him heard him stumble and fall. He had been hit by a bullet which severed the artery in his left thigh, and blood was pumping from the wound in great gouts. He was half pulled, half carried back into the dressing-station, where he said quietly, "Don't carry me down. I don't want any of your stretcher-bearers hit." Then he died.

Before the war, Bridges, then a colonel, had been Chief of Staff of Australia's military forces and then Inspector-General. In that position he had laid out the establishment of the expeditionary force and gave it the title Australian Imperial Force, the AIF, a title that held through two wars. Bridges' loss was a blow, but such blows were being dealt all along the line. Junior and field officers fell alongside their men, the flow of casualties was continuous, and the procession of wounded being led or helped or carried down to the beach was endless.

It was astonishing that, given the frightful casualty rate and the bad and constantly deteriorating conditions, morale stayed high and men found humour and even inspiration. At a kind of domestic level there were the terraces of shelters which began to grow on the reverse slopes of the hillsides, the seaward-facing slopes. Although they were still open to artillery and mortar bombardment, they offered some rest from the continual rifle and machine-gun fire. Men dug into the rockbound soil, scraping shallow caves, shielding them with scraps of sacking or tarpaulin or anything they could find to screen out weather and other men's eyes. They built whole tenement structures like that,

stepped up the hillsides in terraces, and those troglodyte slums were as close as the Anzacs could move to comfort and safety.

Even then, death could come to them quickly, and not only from enemy action. There was a day when troops came blinking from their shelters and crowded the terraces to watch an air fight in the open sky above them. The fascinated men, craning their necks, massed so closely around the rickety shelters that the terraces began to crumble and collapse beneath them; men and shelters, rocks and loose soil fell together, and there were casualties where there should have been some rest and relief.

New Zealand's Lieutenant-Colonel William Malone was a London-born New Zealander, a 56-year-old lawyer and a stickler for discipline and cleanliness. He had taken Quinn's Post with his men of the Wellington Infantry Battalion and at once began a general clean-up of his area while maintaining both vigilance and strength of defence. He introduced the idea of using blankets as sun screens which could be brailed up at night like any veranda screen at home, and he was instrumental in getting heavy iron plates sent forward, loopholed plates which could be set up in sandbagged parapets and used as protective firing points to counter-snipe the Turkish snipers. Wire netting came into its own, too, in a number of places close enough for Turkish grenades to be lobbed. Wooden frames were made, covered with wire netting and then erected on a steep angle over the vulnerable trenches so that the hand bombs rolled down and away.

For the men and the junior officers, the business of Gallipoli was a straightforward enough matter of survival, of doing what soldiers have always done at close quarters with the enemy. For their seniors and for the politicians behind them, the Dardanelles campaign was a tangle of politics, personal ambition and pride and the conflicting interests of the generals and admirals. The differences of opinion between Easterners and Westerners had grown yet more marked in London, and even men who had supported Winston Churchill in his drive for the

ABOVE AND BELOW

In 1914, the seagoing side of the two-year-old Royal Flying Corps broke away and became the Royal Naval Air Service; the air above the Dardanelles was subsequently ruled almost exclusively by young naval fliers. Lieutenant-Commander C.R. Samson, trained in the RFC and the first Royal Navy officer to hold an air command, was given an establishment of 30 seaplanes, and the oil tanker *Ark Royal* was converted to carry them. However, when the planes were uncrated in Egypt before being taken aboard the carrier, only five were serviceable; the rest were cannibalised for enough parts to put together a dozen more over a period of several weeks.

After the Gallipoli landings, Samson and his men operated from a short airstrip on Cape Helles, their seaplanes modified as amphibians, but they were so much under the Turkish guns there that they withdrew to the little offshore island of Tenedos. The planes were primitive wooden constructions, covered in chemically stiffened cloth, capable of only about 75 miles an hour, difficult and dangerous to fly and with no fixed weapons. Samson's pilots flew armed with a revolver and equipped only with binoculars and either a lifebelt or an empty petrol can as a buoy if they were forced into the sea. Observers carried rifles, charts and a watch – and most of those observers were light-weight midshipmen to ease the burden of takeoffs.

While the aircraft were used essentially for reconnaissance and photographic survey, Samson's men extended observation into attack. They began by dropping steel darts – which wobbled so badly in descent that they usually landed sideways and did little damage. *Ark Royal's* fitters and armourers then devised ways of hanging small bombs or mortar shells fitted with flights onto the sides of the aircraft so that observers could release them by tripwire. These early bombing raids not only caused damage and harassment but also had a strong effect on Allied morale.

Meanwhile, under the surface of the Dardanelles, submarines of the British, French and Australian navies harried enemy shipping. As early as December 1914 the Turkish battleship *Messudieh* had been sunk by the little British submarine B11, whose captain, Lieutenant Norman Holbrook, won the first Victoria Cross awarded to a submariner. On April 25, the day of the Anzac landing, the Australian submarine AE2, commanded by Lieutenant-Commander H.G. Stoker, RN, passed through the Narrows and sank an enemy ship in the Sea of Marmara. She operated there for another five days until, after a ferocious fight with a Turkish torpedo boat, she was sunk on April 30.

By then, more of the new E class submarines were in action. E14 created havoc among ships moving supplies and reinforcements down the Dardanelles, and E11 sailed up to Constantinople, where she torpedoed a merchantman, paralyzed shipping in the port and caused near panic among the city's population.

By the end of July the submarine fleet had to contend with a massive wire net strung right across the Narrows and hanging more than 60 metres down to the bottom. E7 was caught in its mesh and was forced to surrender after a murderous two-hour fight. But E11 and E14 found a seabed hollow below the end of the net, scraped through and – with E2 later – shelled reinforcement staging areas, sank several transports and the battleship *Barbarossa Harradin* and a collier berthed alongside the Constantinople arsenal. Lieutenant G. D'Oyley Hughes from E11 performed the astonishing feat of swimming ashore and blowing up a railway viaduct.

When Gallipoli was evacuated, the squadron of seaplanes was dispersed and the underwater arm withdrew to the Mediterranean. Of a total of 13 Allied submarines that had operated in the Sea of Marmara and the Dardanelles, eight were destroyed, including Australia's AE2. Both above and below the awful struggle at Gallipoli, these new systems of warfare had brought new standards of engineering, photography, navigation and gunnery. And, as in the land battles, it became commonplace to see, in the air and below the waves, glowing examples of ingenuity and great bravery.

Submarine AE2 loses a towline during its voyage from Australia to the Dardanelles.

Prime Minister Herbert Asquith

David Lloyd George

THE DARDANELLES COMMITTEE

In the first five weeks of the Dardanelles campaign, the Allies suffered more than 60,000 casualties. Available medical resources in the Middle East – military and civilian hospitals at Mudros, in Egypt and on Malta – were close to exhaustion. On June 4, the British and French launched a massive attack against the village of Krithia; it was a victory of sorts, but the sudden crush of nearly 5,000 Allied casualties in one day led to the formation of a 12-man committee in London to review the situation.

Under the chairmanship of the Liberal Prime Minister, Herbert Asquith, the Dardanelles Committee included as diverse – and contentious – a body of soldiers and politicians as could have been found. Among them was Arthur Balfour, a past Conservative Prime Minister who had recently succeeded Winston Churchill as First Lord of the Admiralty. Sure to be at odds with Balfour was David Lloyd George, Minister for Munitions and a senior Liberal who would replace Asquith as Prime Minister in 1916. Another leading committee member was Viscount Grey, Foreign Minister and the man largely responsible for the founding of Albania out of the chaos of the 1912–13 Balkan Wars. Along the table sat Andrew Bonar Law, a staunch Conservative and, as Colonial Secretary, likely to consider the interests of the Anzacs; with him was the Under-Secretary for the Colonies, the Earl of Selborne.

Winston Churchill, who had resigned from the Admiralty in May, was a leading architect of the Dardanelles campaign; his views were balanced by an earlier First Lord, the Earl of Crewe. Great power and presence surrounded Horatio Herbert, Lord Kitchener of Khartoum, Secretary of State for War, who often clashed with another committee member, Lord Curzon, once Viceroy of India. Rounding out this distinguished assemblage was the Marquis of Lansdowne, himself a former Viceroy of India, and yet another lord, Edward Henry Carson,

Attorney-General, leader of the Ulster Unionists and the man credited with persuading 70,000 Irishmen to enlist in Britain's cause.

Such a committee could hardly be expected to make unanimous or speedy decisions, and yet they had only three choices: complete abandonment of the campaign; massive reinforcement in an attempt to break out of the two bridgeheads; or simply to rebuild General Sir Ian Hamilton's forces to their original strength and let him get on with it as best he could. Kitchener's immediate preference was for that third choice. Churchill argued passionately for the second option – the strongest possible effort – saying, "There never was a great subsidiary operation of war in which a more complete harmony of strategic, political and economic advantages has combined. Through the Narrows of the Dardanelles and across the ridges of the Gallipoli Peninsula lie some of the shortest paths to a triumphant peace." This was typically Churchillian rhetoric, but it matched the public mood of interest and confidence in the Gallipoli front. At that point, no one on the committee favoured abandonment.

In the event, the middle course – modest reinforcement – won out. And General Hamilton had two extra divisions on the way to him before mid-August. Yet by October, the ghastly blood-letting and detestable stalemate led the committee to advocate withdrawal.

The Dardanelles Committee was disbanded in November 1915. But in August 1916 a royal commission was appointed to seek answers to the many questions raised by the conduct of the campaign. That commission's two reports, in 1917 and 1918, stated bluntly that the operation had been ill conceived, inept in its execution, vain in the expenditure of valuable lives and commendable only for the heroism of the troops and the wisdom of General Sir Charles Monro in advocating withdrawal. It was hardly a tribute to the High Command or to the decisions of the Dardanelles Committee.

Winston Churchill

assault on Gallipoli were now having second thoughts. It is true that there had been a great swell of popular feeling for the brave actions on the peninsula, and the Anzacs in particular had been widely praised, but the more sober facts available at the upper levels of government and the army did not make for pleasing reading.

The army had been put ashore to do what the navy had been unable to do – to drive back the Turks on the peninsula so that warships could move up the Dardanelles to Constantinople and open the waterway to Russia. That the navy had then bungled the point of impact of the Anzac landing was past history; that there had been – and still were – bitter fights between and within the two services was regrettable but had to be lived with. The real matter of importance in this mid-year period was whether or not the campaign was getting anywhere. Despite a deal of public enthusiasm and the decision to send out three more British divisions and to expand the fleet in Gallipoli's waters, there were already voices beginning to advocate a withdrawal. Indeed, "Jackie" Fisher resigned as First Sea Lord and walked out of the Admiralty in protest at Winston Churchill's determination to have his own way. Fisher wrote powerfully to Churchill, "YOU ARE BENT ON FORCING THE DARDANELLES AND NOTHING WILL TURN YOU FROM IT – NOTHING. I know you so well!" Fisher's action was one of the precipitating factors in bringing down the government of Prime Minister Herbert Asquith, in putting in its place a coalition government and in forcing Churchill's resignation from the Admiralty, although he held a place on the newly formed Dardanelles Committee.

Throughout these manoeuvrings in London, fighting went on at Gallipoli, men dying and being wounded all the time. By July there had been close to 60,000 casualties among the Allied troops and probably about the same number amoung the Turks. Hamilton had already asked for replacements and reinforcements and, most urgently, for artillery shells, principally for use at Cape Helles. At that time he had on the peninsula eight fighting divisions, none at full strength – four of them British, two French and two Anzac. To the three new divisions already promised, Kitchener now offered to add another two. Hamilton, naturally enough, accepted.

When they arrived, Hamilton would have something more than an adventurous expeditionary force under command, he would have an army of thirteen divisions, about 180,000 men, and the supplies and ammunition for it. Much of that matériel was being sent at the expense of the armies in France and Flanders; for if there was a deadlock at Gallipoli, the situation in Europe was coming to be recognised as a ghastly stalemate. A cursory study of the maps showed that in the Dardanelles a determined and properly mounted offensive had very little distance to go to achieve success. Kitchener, ever a realist, had looked at his maps and his supply tables. For the moment, Gallipoli was where the action was to be.

New ships were to be sent out, too: landing-barges made to Fisher's design, a flotilla of monitors – flat bottomed gun platforms – and a range of supporting ships and seaplane carriers, for there was now a growing air fleet for both observation and bombing.

Meantime, as these quite massive reinforcements were being assembled and their move to Gallipoli begun, there was no question in Hamilton's mind of any sort of temporary stand-down, of an easing-off period till he was at peak strength. At Cape Helles the British and French fought bitter actions, costly and strategically valueless. And at Anzac, with no major actions, the cost in men was unremittingly high, a debit figure made up of bullet and shrapnel strike, of a variety of illness and disease, of simple bone-weariness and malnutrition combined and – perhaps as dangerous as all the rest – a growing feeling of uselessness, of despair.

There was worse to come.

HOME WAS
NEVER LIKE THIS

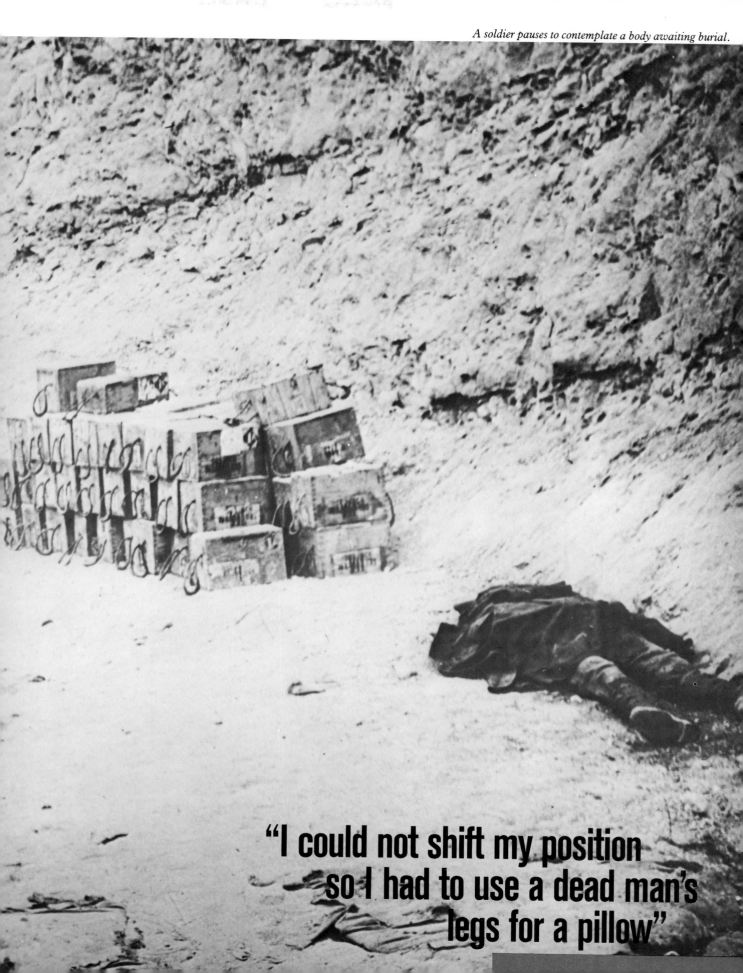

"I could not shift my position so I had to use a dead man's legs for a pillow"

MAKING DO

From the moment they landed at Anzac Cove, the soldiers had to dig and build to establish some sort of protection and living space for themselves. With the entrenching tools and two empty sandbags that each man carried with him, trenches were hastily dug and sandbag parapets erected. It was hard work, as Private Leslie Lott noted in his diary. "To start our trenches," he wrote, "we had to be on our stomach and scratch with anything at all, mostly entrenching tool blade without the handle, for to stand up to dig would have been a sudden exit."

As the campaign wore on, the hillsides became pitted with dugout shelters shielded with sandbags and finished with any available scrap material; bully beef boxes packed with sand made useful steps or walls. Men crawled into these caves to do some of the things that were almost normal—boil a billy, darn socks, lie fully flat and sleep, write a letter home, or prepare a snack, though the millions of flies that infested the peninsula made the eating of it difficult. Trooper Ion Idriess, later to become a best-selling author, described his experience after opening a tin of jam: "I wrapped my overcoat over the tin and gouged out the flies, then spread the biscuit, held my hand over it and drew the biscuit out of the coat. But a lot of flies flew into my mouth and beat about inside. I nearly howled with rage. Of all the bastards of places this is the greatest bastard in the world."

There was no provision for any sort of field canteen, no place where men could buy small luxuries, no entertainment apart from what the men could make for themselves amid the constant shellfire from the Turks. Their one relaxation was to swim in the sea, and that was hazardous. C.E.W.Bean noted on June 23:"One shell today hit a man in the water and took off his arm—at least it was hanging by a thread and he came out of the water holding it. It didn't stop the bathing." Life went on somehow.

At Quinn's Post, Trooper A.M.Maxwell watches for his chance to take a sniping shot at Dead Man's Ridge. Sniping was made safer by the use of the periscope rifle (right, top), an Anzac invention of mirrors and boxwood and wire which allowed the sniper to aim and fire without exposing himself. Bottom: Gunners serve a well-camouflaged artillery piece, possibly a British 18-pounder field gun.

Australians and Maoris haul a water tank up to Plugge's Plateau. Water was brought from Egypt.

A fatigue party carries 18-pounder shells to a gun position. With few pack animals and little other transport, the men had to carry most things themselves.

A dispatch rider gallops on a precarious mission from Suvla Bay to Anzac Cove.

Soldiers at work in the open-air bomb factory at Anzac. Empty food tins were filled with scraps of barbed wire, shrapnel and explosive.

Washing hangs from makeshift lines as Diggers take a rest from battle in their dugout shelters on the seaward slope of a hillside. Though still open to artillery shelling and mortar bombing, the shelters offered some protection from machine-gun and rifle fire.

A spotter picks out a target with a periscope while the sniper waits to take a quick shot over the top of the trench. The periscope rifle later combined the two operations.

Stretcher-bearers perform their endless task (above), while the Digger pictured below carries his wounded mate to the dressing station, together with his own equipment.

Anzacs in a captured Turkish deep sap display a casually observed military style in their uniforms.

Ignoring the risk of shrapnel or gunfire, soldiers frolic in the sea. Everyone from General Birdwood (inset) down was eager to get cool and clean as often as possible. Right: Casually attired Diggers take a well-earned break at Gallipoli.

Left: Captain Phil Fry, later killed at Hill 60, Gallipoli, leans against the trench wall while his companion rests in the background.

SPLINTER
VILLA

Top: Sergeant C. A. Masters and his mate cook a meal for themselves, "making a dish you don't hear of there," Sergeant Masters wrote to his family at Elsternwick, Victoria, "rissoles with bully beef and onions." Masters was killed in France in November 1916. Above: A Digger takes a sponge bath with a dish of brackish water; keeping clean was virtually impossible. Left: Recycled boxes and a wooden barrel furnish and ornament the aptly named Splinter Villa, one of the makeshift homes erected by the Diggers at Anzac.

4

SPRING AND SUMMER SLAUGHTER

When the Anzacs charged the Turks at Lone Pine, they found the trenches roofed with heavy timbers; the battle was fought hand to hand in darkness underground. At the Nek, through error, wave after wave of Light Horsemen charged to certain death.

The land was as much of an enemy as the Turks. Ancient and implacable, rough-ribbed and surfaced with cutting edges, the land opposed the invading armies as harshly as any human enemy.

At the toe of the peninsula a ridge lay athwart the incomer's path about eight kilometres from the toe's tip, a ridge dominated by the height of Achi Baba. Into that double-shouldered crest the Turkish guns and observation posts were dug, looking down over a tight system of strongpoints and rifle pits and trenches to the plains below, where the Allied troops had gained perhaps half the ground from sea to ridge. Achi Baba had been the first objective of the Allied landing at Cape Helles. It had not been reached at any time.

Northwards, at Anzac, that high point could be seen, but only as one of many. The country north of Achi Baba ran up and down and was transversely cut in a succession of narrow valleys and jagged rises, the overall pattern of the sharpest high points running diagonally from right down to left. Above the Narrows stood the bulk of Kilid Bahr; behind that, over the village of Maidos, the land lifted again and then swept down and up to the edged mass of

Gurka kukri, a heavy-backed killing knife with a strong ritual attached to its use. In the back of the scabbard are two small knives used for delicate skinning, for eating and for personal hygiene.

the Sari Bair range. From that great loom of land the eminence of Chunuk Bair looked down in all directions, towards the cape, down to the Narrows and over the lower hills towards Anzac Cove. And still further back along the peninsula the ridges lined across the country in a double rank till their foothills slid away towards a salt lake, not totally dry, and then the rounded sweep of Suvla Bay.

The land between and below the ridges was never easy going, was not open tracts of country like the flower-filled, corn and olive patches of the Cape Helles area. It was as roughly broken as crumpled metal, as likely to cut and fracture, and it offered a succession of sheer faces and back-breaking drops. From the higher rock points and slabs the sun beat back during the heat of the day, and when the light began to fail, the deep shadows brought a chill and the added danger of unseen crevices and gullies. All the major heights and many of the lesser ones were controlled by the Turks, who poured fire from them continuously. Together, Turkish soldier and Turkish land fought the Anzacs, the British, French, Indian and Gurkha troops, held them in check and inflicted terrible wounds on them. It was planned to change all that in August.

The genesis of the plan was in May, when Lieutenant-Colonel Arthur Skeen, an Indian Army officer who was Birdwood's chief of staff, proposed an attack northwards out of Anzac designed to scale and seize the heights of Chunuk Bair. Birdwood asked for reinforcements of a division and an extra brigade so that he could carry such an attack through.

It was a good plan developed from good intelligence and well established and tight co-operation between Australians, New Zealanders and the navy, and Hamilton was initially in favour of it. Then he was offered those extra divisions by Kitchener and began to look for something on a grander scale, some way of justifying the size of the reinforcements. He asked Birdwood for a new and more substantial plan to include three new divisions – and the Suvla Plan came to being. Birdwood and his staff saw it as meaning a new and subsidiary landing on the peninsula, further north, at Suvla Bay. The troops put ashore there would thrust inland and link up with what Birdwood understood would be the main assault, the one Skeen had originally planned to come out of the Anzac positions. The objective would be to seize the Chunuk Bair ridge and thus dominate the entire area above Anzac and the other side of the peninsula, above the Narrows. So far, so good.

The problems began when the expanded version of the original plan was altered and then the alteration was amended and the amendment changed. The problems were compounded by Hamilton's fetish about security, so that essentials of the final operational plan were withheld by him from all but his closest staff.

With the new divisions on the way, with some of them already aboard their transports in Mudros harbour, the simplicity and single-mindedness of Lieutenant-Colonel Skeen's basic plan had developed into a triple-headed affair, a major and complex interlinking of moves which depended on good information, efficient communications, and comprehensive briefings. Its new complexity did not detract from its bold intelligence, from its theme of pressing the enemy from Suvla in the north, from Cape Helles in the south and from the Anzac flank. It was adventurous and with great potential for success, but it needed clear and cohesive organisation and command. The secrecy at Hamilton's headquarters about the amendments to the plan hardly allowed that.

What was worse, Kitchener would not release from the Western Front either of the senior generals Hamilton wanted for the Suvla operation. The man he got was General Sir Frederick Stopford, who had last been effective in any senior position when, in 1899, he had been military secretary to General Sir Redvers Buller in the first phases of the Boer War. Stopford's experience in the field had been in Egypt and the Sudan, well before the turn of the century, and he had never commanded troops in battle. When he was appointed to command the Suvla operation he was 61 years old, had been in poor health and had been living in retirement for five

The "monkey" made from a deloused Turkish shell is raised on the improvised pile-driver during the construction of Anzac's most substantial pier, constructed under the supervision of Lieutenant Stan Watson (below).

ANZAC'S PIERS:

THE ONLY WAY IN OR OUT

There was not much more than two square kilometres of open beach, long and narrow, and all of it under the guns of the enemy. The shoreline curved in a gentle arc, with the rocky outcrop of Ari Burnu at its northern end and the headland known as Hell Spit to the south. When the first troops waded ashore on April 25, no one expected major problems in landing reinforcements, or in supplying the invasion force. But the men were quickly pinned down, and throughout the ordeal on Gallipoli, this bloodsoaked little strip of sand was the only way in or out for the Anzacs.

On that first crucial day, a barge, abandoned under the sheets of Turkish fire, drifted inshore and became, by chance, the first of a truly remarkable series of piers and jetties fingering out from Anzac Cove into the Aegean Sea. Without them, a military stalemate might well have turned into a catastrophe of epic proportions.

Within little more than a week of the landing, two large dumps of supplies had been assembled, one on the stretch of Anzac Cove that became known as Brighton Beach, the other at the southern end of the cove. Yet it was obvious that a proper pier was needed to supply the 15,000 men clinging desperately to the beachhead.

Towards the end of May, a party of the 2nd Field Company, Royal Australian Engineers, under the temporary command of the young Signals officer Lieutenant Stan Watson, set to with a will to push a sturdy wooden pier far out into the cove. Suitable timber was obtained from one of the transport ships. The problem of how to drive the piles was solved with traditional Australian ingenuity. Watson explained: "I had observed an 8-inch or 9-inch naval armour-piercing shell from the Turkish cruiser *Barbarossa* lying on the slope of one of the gullies and decided that it would do the job if deloused and adapted for the purpose. This I did with some fear, and it became the 'monkey' of a fabricated pile-driver; it was filled with shrapnel pellets to add to its weight."

Watson and his men worked continuously during daylight hours in clear sight of the enemy. Every so often a Turkish artillery shell would blossom hideously among the labouring men; rifle and machine-gun fire hailed down without cease. Nonetheless, in scarcely three weeks, on June 18, Watson's Pier was finished: it was a masterwork of combat engineering, 64 metres long and holding 19 bays for boats and barges with a tide depth in the seaward bays of over four metres. Though Watson's was the biggest

and best built, there were numerous other piers and jetties. At the start of the August offensive, it was decided to construct a rough pier at North Beach, behind the rise of Ari Burnu and out of sight of enemy artillery observers. That pier – called William's – became one terminus of a light tramway traversing the length of the beach to connect the flanks of the landing force. Lorries also roared along the beach carrying ammunition and supplies brought in to the piers. In time, yet another major pier – Walker's – was thrust out from North Beach. And now, on a good night, the piers and jetties made it possible for as many as 6,000 men to come ashore with their equipment and supplies.

By the time of the evacuation in December, the piers and several grounded vessels were in constant use. For the final night of the withdrawal – December 19 – a foot-walk was run out from the beach to the sunken steamer *Milo*, and streams of men hurried along the boards to the rescue boats moored to the hulk. Without these fingers of salvation, there is no telling how many of the Anzacs would have survived. But it most certainly would not have been the 20,000 brave, bloody and exhausted men who made it out to the safety of the fleet on those last two nights.

Watson's Pier juts out from a cluttered stretch of Anzac Cove.

A damaged Watson's Pier in the aftermath of November storms.

years. Even so, the Suvla Plan had enough men, enough ships, enough artillery ammunition to offer it a strong chance of success, and August shaped as the month that might change the course of the Dardanelles campaign.

For the raw troops on the transports in Mudros harbour it was a period of knowing where they were but not where they were going or why. Company commanders, even the colonels who commanded their regiments, were kept largely in the dark about the details of the assault; no maps were issued, and there were no proper briefings. For the men of the British 13th Division, there was the fear and confusion of being hurried ashore by night at Anzac and literally hidden there to await the time for the break-out. There was not the shipping to carry them as well as the rest of the Suvla striking force in one lift, and it was essential that the Turks should not become aware of any build-up, of any mass of troops arriving to herald an imminent attack. The 13th Division was fresh from Britain, replacement battalions for those lost in the carnage of France and Flanders; they were moved ashore in darkness and hustled into the darkness of the places prepared for them.

That preparation had imposed a most arduous task on the men of Anzac. Not only did they have to go on fighting, but when they were out of the trenches, ostensibly to rest, their endless fatigues were multiplied by the need to find concealment for those extra battalions who would wait there, hidden, until the time came for the Suvla attack. So Anzacs came from the stress of action to hard labour – digging more trenches and tunnels, widening tracks, covering over gullies, stockpiling more supplies, more water, and all of it done under fire at night so that the overlooking Turks would not suspect the reasons. Sick and weary Anzacs, new and inexperienced young Tommies, old hands of the 29th Division, French and Indian and Gurkha soldiers, Royal Marines and sailor-soldiers of the Royal Naval Divisions – at the beginning of August they were all, more than 100,000 of them, waiting to become part of the Suvla Plan.

But by then there was more than one version of the plan in the minds of key commanders. Birdwood, commanding the Anzacs, still believed that the main attack would come from his front, with his New Zealand and Australian division sweeping round the foothills of the Sari Bair range to seize the heights of the Chunuk Bair ridge. For him, the Suvla landing was a support to his northerly drive, and any attack at Cape Helles was no more than a feint to keep the Turks occupied. But for Hamilton, commander-in-chief, both the Cape Helles and the Anzac attack were feints designed to distract attention from the Suvla landing, after which the Anzac force would link up to form a new, wide and deeper front from which a last great push could be made to cut across the peninsula. So obsessed was Hamilton with the need for security in this whole action that the details of the operation orders were not passed to Birdwood's staff – who had originated the whole idea – until less than two days before the jump-off.

Just as bad was the division of opinion that arose between Birdwood and his subordinate commanders about the details of their own immediate operation. Birdwood was convinced of the need to prepare another diversion for the Turks on their own front and to suck into one area as many enemy forces as possible from the north to lessen the danger to his sweeping movement round the base of the heights. There was a strong divergence of opinion about the best place for this diversion – if, indeed, there was any real need for it. It had to be in strength to be effective as a diversion, and Birdwood could not have felt fully confident of its being anything more than that. He wrote in his diary, "In case of complete failure all that could happen could be that the attacking force would fall back on its original trenches. The continuous fighting which would in any case take place must help the attack elsewhere." The men he chose for this diversion were those of the excellent 1st Australian Infantry Division, the heart of Australia's army. The place he chose was known by a most evocative name and one which was to become one of the best-known battle honours in military history. It was called Lone Pine.

Diggers rest in a gully on the way to Lone Pine. The attack began at 5:30 p.m. on August 6.

At ten minutes to four in the afternoon of August 6, Britain's acclaimed 29th Division clawed across the parapets of its trenches at Cape Helles and went forward against the Turks. The division was diminished already by almost two hours of punishing enemy artillery fire as it waited. Across the range, to the north, there was also the boom and roar of gunfire, the third day of a spasmodic barrage laid down to cut the Turkish barbed wire and deliberately kept spasmodic to lessen the suspicion of an attack in the making. Under the lofting shells the 1st Australian Infantry Division waited in deep trenches and in the saps and tunnels that had been pushed forward underground in preparation for this day. Above, the late afternoon sun glared down through black and yellow smoke and rising clouds of dust; below, the men crouched sweating and reeking in claustrophobic tunnels, and the whole earth trembled and threatened to swallow them up. Young officers squinted to see the hands on watches move around to half-past five.

Between those temporary tombs and the enemy lay a slab of plateau, about 100 metres of scrubby ground rising very slightly on the Turkish side. There was a clear field of fire across it, but the Turks had some major advantages. They overlooked the whole position from the rise called Baby 700 and they had fortified the place strongly. Moreover, the ground behind them was sheltered with a wide hollow known as the Cup, in which reserves could be held.

On the Western Front, night patrols to reconnoitre enemy lines had become common, and prisoners were taken for interrogation and information. But this had never been possible at Gallipoli. The closeness of the opposed positions, the roughness of the terrain and the fact that Anzacs almost always had to fight uphill had put night patrolling out of consideration. So, for the Australians there was only the plateau itself to be seen, that and the barely visible, fire-spitting trench-line on the far side.

At 5:30 p.m. on August 6, with the sun flattening and the shadows beginning to stretch, the artillery barrage stopped and there was a long second of silence. Then the whistles blew and the shouts began and men moved up and out of the ground. The ends of sandbagged tunnels were pushed open, men leapt across the crumbling edges of trenches, and behind them 85

The tussocky ground barely reveals the loopholes in the Turkish covered trench line running across the top of the picture. Anzacs at Lone Pine found the trenches a surprise, but not impregnable.

the second wave moved up onto the fire-steps and the third wave rose from the trench floor and crouched ready.

In seconds the plateau was filled with running men, stumbling, sometimes falling on the broken ground, bayoneted rifles held high, the steel catching the orange sunlight through the smoke and dust haze which lay all around. Ahead gaped the craters of the three underground mines which had been blown earlier that afternoon to offer them some cover in their naked assault, and then the sharp tatters of the Turkish wire, cut but still a menace where the chopped lengths of barbs lay tangled in the low scrub. Further ahead were the Turkish trenches, and when the Australians reached them – with few casualties – they found the unexpected.

The Turkish front line was no open trench. It was roofed with heavy baulks of timber, well packed down and covered with a solid layer of sunbaked earth. Just below that roof lip were loopholes, rifle and machine-gun barrels spitting from them. There was only one way the enemy could be reached in that front line, and that was to go down there after him. So the attack developed in two ways. As the follow-

up waves broke out into no man's land, they saw the men of the first wave lined along the far edge of the plateau. C.E.W. Bean, the official Anzac historian, wrote that they resembled "a crowd not unlike that lining the rope around a cricket field." Men stooped and knelt to poke rifle muzzles into gun ports and empty their magazines or lay alongside them to stab down with their bayonets. Some of them found the few places where the roofing had gaps in it or ganged together to wrench some of the beams away so that they could leap down into the heat and darkness below. Others simply ran on across the roofing timbers and beyond to the reserve trenches. There, where the ground sloped away towards the Cup, no head cover had been built. The Turks, rushing up into the line, jamming together in the narrow communication trenches, looked up and saw the long silhouettes of the Australians above them and the wicked glint and flash of the bayonets.

In the covered front-line trench, there was a tangled mass of men below the ground as more and more of the attackers forced their way in. Turk and Australian packed together in the dark and stinking trenches, so close that the only way to gain room was to kill an enemy and take his space. The timbered roof caught and flung the hideous echoes of shots and screams, and the

dead and wounded began to pile in the narrow places so that the second and third waves leapt down onto a soft and bloody carpet, stumbling in the sudden loss of light to avoid running on the wounded. Every corner, every angle was a danger point, with Turkish riflemen on the reverse side firing point-blank. There was no room for a man to use the length of his rifle as a shaft of his bayonet; he had to run with the rifle held almost vertical, check at a corner, leap around and drop the bayonet point as he went, firing on the run and plunging point-forward into the Turks. Some men discarded their rifles entirely and went into that nauseous warren like infantry of old, bayonets used as swords, and there were Turks fighting back just as viciously, some of them swinging entrenching tools like battleaxes. There were even places where men grappled together weaponless, fingers digging and gouging, fists hammering as they staggered and rolled on the slippery floor.

James Croker was a Devon man who migrated to the Kalgoorlie goldfields in 1910 and enlisted in the 11th West Australian Battalion when war broke out. He had been lightly wounded on the day of the landing and again in late May, but he was among those who fought at Lone Pine. He said afterwards, "We was like a mob of ferrets in a rabbit-hole. I was blood all down the side of me face where the bottom part of me right ear got took off by a bullet. Might have been one of ours for all I know. And I was blood up to me other wrist from where it splashed out of a Johnny when I put the bayonet in. I never reckoned to get out of there. It was one long grave, only some of us was still alive in it."

Above them the afternoon darkened into evening and the battle raged. In the south, at Cape Helles, the British and French advance was checked, and there was a merciless struggle for ground beneath a sky racked and tormented by the continuing barrage and counter-barrage. The slopes of Achi Baba, still unattainable to the Allies, were ripped and fragmented by the gunfire. The dust and smoke were thick and acrid on the battlefield. Communication with forward units was lost, field-telephone lines could not last in the steel rain that fell, and visual signals could not be seen as evening came on to add to the day's gloom. The attack was pressed hard and well, but the impetus was lost; it slowed its foward move and stopped and became a static killing contest in the dark.

The darkness made little difference at Lone Pine. The appalling battle went on below ground and in the open communication trenches all the way back to the Cup. Staring 87

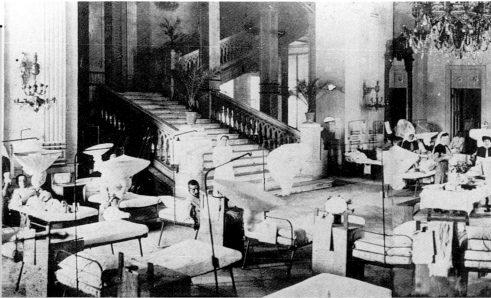

BITTER MEDICINE

Florence Nightingale would not have felt out of place on Gallipoli. There were dead and wounded from the moment of landing, and the one casualty clearing station that went ashore with 1st Anzac Corps headquarters on April 25 had a complement of only 63 men. While each unit provided stretcher-bearers and some medical staff, the mounting numbers of unburied dead and of wounded awaiting treatment often became unmanageable, especially after heavy fighting.

What mud would do on the Western Front, the fly did on Gallipoli; it became an implacable enemy. The combination of open wounds, heat, dirt, lice, fleas, lack of water, an unsatisfactory diet and fatigue were all compounded by fly-borne diseases. There was no chance to bury many of the dead of either side; while strict control of hygiene was imposed wherever possible, latrines were crude; Turkish hygiene was less controlled, and human faeces were added to the food scraps and mule droppings that littered the lines. And when wounded and sick men were evacuated to Mudros, conditions there were only better in that the men were out of range of Turkish guns. Even the nurses and doctors on Mudros were savaged by the prevalent illnesses of dysentery, diarrhoea and gastro-enteritis. The flies were with them too.

That so much was done for the ill and the wounded was largely due to the unremitting efforts of Colonel Neville Howse, Chief Medical

Officer of the 1st Australian Division. As a young lieutenant in South Africa, Howse galloped into Boer fire to rescue a fallen trumpeter and treat his wounds and was honoured with the Victoria Cross for his gallantry. At Gallipoli he was the driving force behind the attempts to cope with the enormous medical problems the Anzacs faced. It was at his insistence that dentists were finally sent to Gallipoli midway through the campaign, and the incinerators he ordered built to burn soiled dressings and other litter were the only useful disposal system on the peninsula. Howse became Director-General of Medical Services for the Australian Military Forces and later, as a federal parliamentarian, Minister for Defence and Health, but it was in the field that his worth was recognised by the men whose lives were saved by his medical skill and organising ability.

There has never been a clear estimate made to show how many of the 10,000 Anzacs who died at Gallipoli were the victims of disease or of the impossibility of treating wounds properly under conditions as bad as any in war. Among the battles fought on that primitive peninsula, none was as unrelenting, as bitterly fought as that by the medical staff. But, like the campaign itself, it was a battle that ended in defeat – yet without loss of honour.

Members of the Australian Army Medical Corps attend to a wounded soldier in a field surgery on Gallipoli.

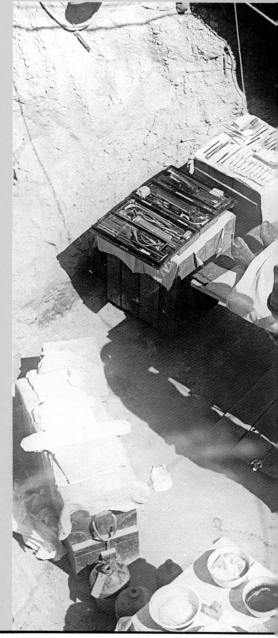

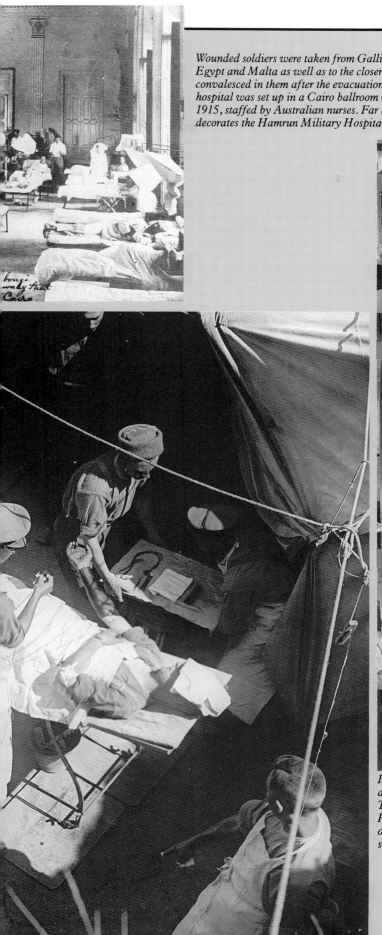

Wounded soldiers were taken from Gallipoli to hospitals in Egypt and Malta as well as to the closer Lemnos, and they convalesced in them after the evacuation. An emergency hospital was set up in a Cairo ballroom (left) in September 1915, staffed by Australian nurses. Far left: A Christmas tree decorates the Hamrun Military Hospital in Valetta, Malta.

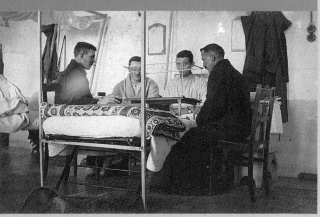

Photographs from the album of Lieutenant N. T. Svensen, a patient in B ward of Hamrun Hospital in Valleta. Top: The ward decorated for Christmas Day. Centre: Recuperating soldiers enjoy dinner in the ward on Boxing Day. Bottom: "The generals studying the situation"; Lieutenant Svensen is on the right.

down into the hollow in the last of the daylight, a loose group of Australians saw enemy reserve troops being rushed into formations, and they ran down the side of the slope, ripping through the astonished Turks and reaching right to their headquarters. But they were unsupported and outnumbered, and the enemy stood firm. The Australians fought there till the last of them was killed. It made no difference to the savagery of the fighting between their corpses in the Cup and the former Turkish front-line trench at Lone Pine.

The same darkness covered the move of Birdwood's troops heading northwards out of Anzac. They proceeded in two columns—on the right, the New Zealanders; on the left, Australians, Indians and Gurkhas—so as to pass the principal features of the land on either side, thereby dividing Turkish fire-power, and to reach the link-up area with Suvla force in less time and on a wider front than one long column.

And further north the Suvla Plan was under way. The aged General Stopford was now in command of IX Corps, a creation of Hamilton's in which he had grouped the new army divisions from Britain—the largely unblooded troops of the 10th (Irish) Division, the 11th and the men of the 13th who had lain hidden at Anzac and then been reshipped north. The plan called for the fighting far to the south at Cape Helles to ensure that no Turkish troops from that area would be shifted northwards and for the Lone Pine diversion to draw towards it whatever reinforcements the Turks had available. The Suvla landing, then, was expected to be a comparatively simple affair, capable of being dealt with by new troops under an aged general's hesitant command. It was believed likely that by mid-morning of August 7 more than 60,000 Allied troops would be successfully fighting less than half their number across the entire Suvla-Anzac area. It was a badly misplaced belief.

The two columns out of Anzac worked their way up grimly defended foothills and along difficult and shot-ridden gullies, and while the obscure and static fight went on down at the cape, while the Australians fought knee-deep in dead at Lone Pine, the northern assault stumbled on, gallantly but doomed.

On the broken slopes of Chunuk Bair, the New Zealanders and the Gurkhas were within reach of the commanding heights, less than a kilometre from the lightly defended summit which was their objective. They were waiting only for their second wave in order to push on and form one jaw of the pincer movement which would clinch the battle. The other jaw was to swing in from Suvla in a carefully timed closing operation.

But at Suvla there was the confusion which was the hallmark of the entire campaign. And General Stopford, unwell, militarily inactive since the Boer War, was not the man to give the incisive commands to end that confusion. Many of his unseasoned troops were landed in the wrong order, many in the wrong place, many in deep water and under growing fire. The landing beaches were thick with men trying to sort themselves out; then, when the move inland began, key points could not be located, the defensive fire became heavier and the timetable was lost. The force struggled off the beaches and onto a mushy section of the salt lake and then up into the rough tilt of the country, savaged all the way by dropping fire from the increasing number of reserves being moved against them. The Turks and their German advisers had awakened to the real facts of the whole operation and had swung the balance of their reserves to the north. The attacking soldiers, largely newcomers to war, were stunned by the rigours of the terrain, by a temperature of more than 35 degrees Celsius, by a shortage of water because of poor supply organisation from beach to fighting front, and by the unexpectedly high casualty rate. Exhausted and dehydrating men, in battle for the first time, made excellent targets for the Turks. The casualty rate was terrifying. The advance slowed and wavered and stopped.

On the other side of the range, the Australians, too, were losing men to heavy fire. Among the most savage losses were those of the

A group of Anzacs pause in one of the covered trenches at Lone Pine after the capture of the Turkish positions.

Australian Light Horse, who formed part of the left-hand assault column. These were the men who in May had volunteered to serve with the Gallipoli force and who left their horses in Egypt and became infantrymen. On August 7, 1915, they became the stuff of legend.

They were positioned in the trenches along Walker's Ridge and at Quinn's Post, looking out on the lift of Baby 700, their objective. There was only one way to reach it – along the narrow death-trap called the Nek, a physical situation which roughly resembled attacking an inverted frying-pan by going up the handle. Still gaitered and bandoliered as horsemen, the men of the 8th Light Horse from Victoria and the 10th from Western Australia – about 600 in all – waited beneath a massive artillery barrage, the standard procedure, expected to crush all opposition into the ground and seldom if ever succeeding. This time there was even less chance, for as the men fidgeted and sweated in their four waves, the barrage stopped seven minutes before the arranged time. Whether it was an accident, a misunderstanding, a matter of unsynchronised watches, no one dared give the signal to advance in case their men were

Dead soldiers line the parapet of a Lone Pine trench. The officer on the right is Major L.J. (later Sir Leslie) Morshead, commander at Tobruk in World War II.

caught out in the open by a final burst of the artillery barrage.

In those seven minutes of agonising silence, the Turks shook themselves clear of the effects of the gunfire, hastily dragged their casualties away and settled behind their weapons. At the end of the seven minutes, precisely on time, the Light Horsemen went to their deaths.

The first wave out of the trenches moved up into solid fire and was shot down on the parapet or, at the most, a metre or two beyond. It was not possible to live in those sheets of steel. The second wave climbed over the dead and ran out into the fence of bullets. The third wave dashed out and ran, stumbling through the new dead, and some fell only short metres away from the hot rifle muzzles of the Turks. Observing officers could see the deadly harvesting of men and were able to stop most of the fourth wave; the rest moved out along a path of dead and dying mates and went down with them.

Troop-Sergeant Bill Sanderson later recounted that he glanced over his shoulder and saw "four men running about 10 yards behind and they all dropped at the same moment." Another Light Horseman said that the attacking men "sank to the ground as though their limbs had become string." C.E.W. Bean, the official observer on the spot, counted the bodies of more than 300 Australians in an area smaller than a tennis court when he led a party back to Gallipoli in 1919. Hardly a man reached as far as the Turkish line. The simple-minded planning which sent in such a frontal assault against a heavily entrenched and heavily gunned position was deplorable, but not unusual at that time in that place. The courage that took the horsemen forward cannot be over-praised. Bean called their action "a deed of self-sacrificing bravery which has never been surpassed in military history."

The patterns of death were shaped in many ways along the peninsula during those August days. None formed the shape of success.

The slaughter at the diversion of Lone Pine dragged on till August 8. The Australians took and held the entire Turkish front line and most of the communication and reserve trenches—

the most significant gain of the whole campaign. They were reversing those positions and, in many cases, barricading trenches part-way along their length, for the fighting had developed into a bomber's war. Sections of trench were held by Turks at one end, Australians at the other; new sections were dug and bays pushed out in the attempt to overlook an enemy position; bombs flew across hastily erected barriers, often enough made of corpses, and the Turks launched counter-attack after counter-attack across the tiny strips of torn ground that lay between trench and reeking trench.

The casualties mounted on both sides until the frenzy slowed and died away and became another piece in the dull mosaic of a hopeless campaign. At Lone Pine the Turks lost 7,000 men; the splendid 1st Australian Infantry Division, 4,600-strong at the outset, lost more than 3,000. In simple comparative terms it was a battle the Australians won. In terms of the campaign, of drawing Turkish arms towards the small sector, it achieved its objective. It may be of some interest to record that the battle which cost 9,000 lives and which was planned as no more than a diversion was obviously recognised as just that by the Turks. In their war diary they called it "The Demonstration."

Two days after the end of Lone Pine, late on August 10, the broad battle stopped—from exhaustion rather than intent, for both sides were drained. At Cape Helles, the fighting had ground to a misery-laden halt with no effective gains having been made. At Suvla, the bold and ingenious plan had become a dreary and disastrous failure, the more poignant because of its great prospect and the nearness of success. In the broken country between Anzac and Suvla, the hope of winning the Dardanelles campaign bled to death. Of more than 60,000 men fighting in those places, 18,000 fell and, in the following two days, 20,000 were evacuated as wounded or sick.

Yet there was still killing to be faced.

Hamilton determined on yet another attack at Suvla, on a huge thrust against the Turks, depending as much on numbers as on any form

Neatly inscribed simple wooden crosses mark the graves of some of the men killed during the May fighting on Gallipoli. At the end of the campaign almost 11,000 Allied dead lay buried, while more than 30,000 more remained unburied on the hills and in the gullies together with the Turkish dead.

of military skill. He had at his disposal yet more new army divisions sent by Kitchener, the 53rd and 54th, the replacement battalions of long-established County regiments from London and the south of England and from Wales. And he had a clear message from Kitchener, too, about the commander at Suvla and his immediate subordinates, Major-General Sir Bryan Mahon, an Irishman commanding the 10th Division, and Major-General F. Hammersley, commanding the 11th. "If you deem it necessary to replace Stopford, Mahon and Hammersley, have you any competent generals to take their place? This is a young man's war and we must have commanding officers who will take full advantage of opportunities which occur but seldom." It was a little late for Kitchener, who had sent Stopford out, to be reminding Hamilton that it was "a young man's war."

General Stopford and a number of his staff were recalled. Command passed to Major-General H. B. de Lisle, of whom Birdwood wrote in a letter to his wife, "He's a real thruster and everyone hates him as he is a brute, with no thoughts for others, rude to everyone and has no principles, but I believe him to be the right man in the right place, and by his brutality I hope he will see things through." On August 21, with 3,000 Anzacs supporting the move, the new assault went in from Suvla.

There were more troops involved in that attack than in any other single battle on the peninsula, but it began badly, became worse and sank into disaster. The men went to their start lines late in the morning, the skies clear and the sun already parching them in yet another day of flat heat. At noon the air became hazy, and as the advance began the haze became a mist, thick and humid, the sun striking a lurid orange through it and the heat becoming a stifling and damp blanket.

In that dim swirl the assaulting force marched across the dry grill of the salt lake, Turkish guns firing down into the opaque mass so that the shrapnel sliced the mist into tatters. Men sank into the shifting, closing blanket unseen from one another, only the screams and cries marking where the wounded lay. As the afternoon wore on, the lowering sun cast no shadows in that deadly mist, and in the last of the daylight the soldiers began to climb up towards an enemy invisible in a bullet-ridden murk.

It was an impossible situation. The Turks, from their heights, had seen the preparation, the move up and the start of the advance and its line before the mist closed in. They simply fired and went on firing in the haze and then into the climbing men as they rose up out of it, stumbling, disoriented and wickedly cut apart by the flying steel. The Turks brought up reserves, almost their last but entirely sufficient for the work of that day; the attack cost more than 5,000 men and gained no ground at all. On the Anzac front, the 3,000 Australians, New Zealanders, British and Gurkhas who were in support struggled on for almost a week without being able to win the single strategic summit for which they fought. The slopes below that peak were thick with unburied dead, for there was no way to stop fighting long enough to perform that human chore.

It was the end of set-piece battles on the peninsula, the end of optimism about the campaign, the end of Hamilton. Almost 50,000 had been bitterly involved in the linked Suvla-Anzac fighting. Of them, more than 22,000 were evacuated in one week, many wounded, many ill, a frightening number suffering from bullet or shrapnel strike and rotten with dysentery as well. There were no beds for them in Middle Eastern hospitals, and those who could stand the journey were shipped directly to England. The magnificent 1st Australian Infantry Division had landed more than 13,000 strong, had taken nearly 8,000 replacements and was now, at the end of August, down to 8,500. An appalling 12,500 brave men lay dead or wounded or too ill to fight—in many cases too sick even to move. The exhausted and tattered remnants of the opposing armies were still for a while. Only the flies were active in the slaughterhouse between Anzac Cove and Suvla Bay.

OFFICIAL WAR ARTISTS

The only artists with the Anzacs on Gallipoli were a few talented men who had enlisted to serve as fighting soldiers. There was little time or opportunity for these men to exercise their talents, but somehow some of them managed to do so, and C.E.W. Bean, Australia's official war correspondent, encouraged them to contribute to *The Anzac Book,* his project to entertain the troops in the field. It was the success of this project that led to the commissioning of official war artists to depict major events of the war and record the conditions of the soldiers.

After the war, Bean led a group back to Gallipoli to gather relics for the proposed Australian War Memorial and to paint, photograph and map the scenes of battle. The artist with the group was George Lambert, the only war artist to be appointed to the rank of honorary captain. At the Nek, where waves of Light Horsemen had charged to their deaths in August 1915, Lambert noted: "This morning I was out at twenty minutes to sunrise to get the effect of light for the charge at the Nek. Very cold, bleak and lonely. The worst feature of this after-battle work is that the silent hills and valleys sit stern and unmoved, callous of the human, and busy only growing bush and sliding earth to hide the scars left by the war-disease."

Gallipoli Wildflowers, painted by George Lambert during his visit to Gallipoli with C.E.W. Bean in 1919.

*Anzac, The Landing. George Lambert's
dramatic re-creation of the scene on April 25,1915.*

*The Charge of the 3rd Light Horse Brigade at the Nek.
Lambert sketched the scene at dawn
to catch the light.*

The Beach at Anzac, by Frank Crozier, shows Anzac Cove from the south with the knoll of Ari Burnu at the northern end. Hastily built jetties allowed the landing of stores stacked on the beach.

"The Australian and New Zealand troops have indeed proved themselves worthy sons of the Empire."

GEORGE R.I.

Frontispiece of The Anzac Book, by Trooper W. Otho Hewett of the Light Horse

Top: Paul Montford's bronze bust of General Sir John Monash, who commanded the 4th Infantry Brigade at Anzac. Bottom: The Man with the Donkey, a bronze by Leslie Bowles portraying Private Simpson and his donkey transporting a wounded soldier.

Sketch from Quinn's Post, one of the topographical sketches in pen and watercolour by Horace Moore-Jones.

Anzac Cove looking towards Achi Baba, Evening, by Moore-Jones. Watson's Pier can be seen in the foreground.

Arrival of the First Wounded from Gallipoli at the 3rd London General Hospital, by George Coates. Coates, who studied art at the National Gallery School in Melbourne, served with the Royal Army Medical Corps at the 3rd London General Hospital at Wandsworth.

A VOICE FROM ANZAC

"FUNNY THING, BILL. I KEEP THINKING I HEAR MEN MARCHING!"

One of Will Dyson's many war cartoons. Dyson worked continuously as an offical war artist from December 1916 till March 1920 and was wounded at Messines and Zonnebeke.

5

AUTUMN MADNESS

"Sickness, the legacy of a desperately trying summer, took heavy toll of the survivors of so many arduous conflicts," wrote General Hamilton. "No longer was there any question of operations on the grand scale." Hamilton was soon to be relieved.

By the beginning of September there was a growing body of opinion among the policy-makers in London that the Dardanelles should be evacuated. It was a part—perhaps an understandable part—of a prevalent feeling of gloom and doom. East of Gallipoli the Russians had yielded hugely to the Austro-German army, losing almost 600,000 men and some thousands of guns; the Italian offensive against the Austrians had been savagely repulsed; the Balkans still teetered uneasily between one side and the other, with Bulgaria about to tip the balance in Germany's favour; on the Western Front men by the hundreds of thousands were being readied for yet another bloodbath before the winter. There seemed little reason for joy or optimism, and certainly Gallipoli offered none.

Hamilton was increasingly criticised for his handling of the campaign—for the horrendous losses he had sustained; for the unduly hopeful tone of his dispatches as against the bloody reality of events. General Stopford, in London after being relieved of his command, had handed in a bitterly critical report of Hamilton's conduct of the campaign; after reading it, Kitchener told the Dardanelles Committee; "There has been considerable criticism of Sir Ian

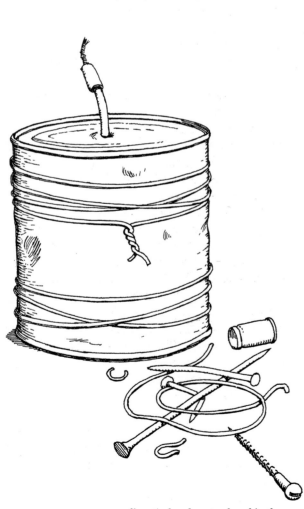

Jam tin bomb as produced in the bomb factory on Anzac Beach.

Hamilton's leadership." He wrote to Hamilton, warning him that there were "reports from Gallipoli criticising the staff and your headquarters and complaining that members of your staff are much out of touch with the troops."

Hamilton, in response, wrote to Kitchener that sickness had taken so many men out of action that he had only 50,000 left to hold more than 21 kilometres of front between Anzac and Suvla. He said, "It appears inevitable that within the next fortnight I shall be compelled to relinquish either Suvla Bay or Anzac Cove, and must also envisage the possibility of a further reduction of my front in the near future into the original Anzac position." Hamilton was unaware that 20,000 more troops were on the way to him following his earlier calls for replacements; neither did he know of the divisions within the Dardanelles Committee, with the Colonial Secretary, Bonar Law, and the Minister for Munitions, Lloyd George, increasingly opposed to continuing the Gallipoli campaign. Yet, while a withdrawal may have been more and more mooted, it was recognised that it would be a drastic move and fraught with great political dangers. So, while it became more frequently talked about and a few senior soldiers sketched out possible systems of evacuation, no one yet moved to make the talk become reality.

At Gallipoli the war went on.

By now, and with the end of the big battles, the whole thing had taken on something of a routine shape. The four months since the landing had produced a crop of Gallipoli veterans, survivors who had mastered the necessary craft and science of staying alive in that most hostile environment. These were men who knew intimately the safest routes to follow, who ducked instinctively at certain places, who even had pet names for Turkish snipers.

The living conditions remained grim, of course. Jack Tarrant, a 21-year-old from Wyong on the New South Wales coast, wrote later, "I have known a loaf of bread to be shared by 32 men. The biscuits had to be soaked overnight to soften them for chewing or for making a kind of porridge. The meat was very salty and the cooks could not do anything to relieve the taste of the salt. The water was always scarce, especially for those men in the front line." Hamilton himself recognised the water situation very well. In one of his dispatches he wrote, "True thirst is a sensation unknown to the dwellers in cool, well-watered England. But at Anzac, when mules with water 'pakhals' arrived at the front, the men would rush up to them in swarms, just to lick the moisture that had exuded through the canvas bags." And later: "Having got from the War Office all that they could give me, I addressed myself to India and Egypt, and eventually I managed to secure portable receptacles for 100,000 gallons, including petrol tins, milk cans, camel tanks, and water bags." Water had been found below ground at Anzac, and bores were sunk and condensers built to clarify it. Lighters came in every night to discharge drinking water in the awkward containers Hamilton had scrounged, but the problem remained that men had to move it by hand up the gullies and ridges to the firing points, and quite a few of them fell to Turkish bullets or shrapnel.

Many of the carriers and the men whose thirst they were sent to ease had been ill and were still unfit. Many of them had been wounded and then returned to active service or had refused to be evacuated in the first place. Many of them went on with the fighting and the fatigues without ever reporting sick; it was to them, perhaps, a little too much like "letting their mates down." They were becoming gaunt because of the poor diet and the effects of debilitating stomach diseases; they suffered from shortness of breath, rapid and sometimes irregular heartbeats, blurred vision, halitosis, lice and a variety of skin infections. Jack Tarrant wrote, "The body-lice gave us a terrible time. Many men were evacuated through the sores caused by the scratching."

Reinforcements arriving fresh from outside looked with some horror on these men, astonished that they could—and did—not only move and fight but laugh. An extract from a rough pencilled letter offers this recipe: "Bash 107 together the contents of a tin of bully beef (might be camel!) with two or three of our standard fido's biscuits. Add a cut up onion if you can buy or otherwise find one and a drop or two of water to glue it all together. Drop a little fat into a dixie-pan or rifle-oil if nothing else and cook together on a fire of broken ammo boxes with a pinch of salt. If no salt, lean across and the sweat of your brow will flavour it all. The end result is a savoury and almost digestible mess we call Grungey." The newcomers who were surprised by laughter amid the horror soon heard the bitter undertones, and it took very little time before they began to look like the old hands. The never-ending Turkish fire soon broke them in.

And while the first tentative discussions about withdrawal were already taking place in London, the fighting went on, small-scale but no less deadly. The fatigues went on, and the pattern of maintaining life and holding to sanity amid madness became something like routine.

The focus of life for the Anzacs was the beach at Anzac Cove, the small and wrong space through which the initial landing and all subsequent traffic passed. From being a faulty foothold it became a way station for everything the invading army needed, a transit camp, a depot, a base station and, of all things, a place for recreation. Between May and August in largely cloudless weather, the cove's waters were placid and warm, sunstruck and inviting. To men who were deeply tired and disgustingly dirty, the invitation was hard to resist, no matter that a combined swim-and-bath meant exposing one's nakedness to Turkish shrapnel.

It was an extraordinarily crowded and busy scene. Boats of all kinds were constantly on the move inshore, to the sturdy length of Watson's Pier, pulled up through the thin surf and onto the beach or against one of the smaller groynes or jetties that had been pushed out. There was a continuous passage to and from the boats — replacements, stores of all kinds, ammunition, water in milk churns and petrol cans, a non-stop inflow of matériel balanced by the outgoing of

the wounded and the sick, off to Mudros or to Egypt or Home or to a neat military graveyard somewhere. As the boxes and bales and bundles came in, they were stacked and piled in growing lines so that the stacks made an area of body-narrow laneways which offered some protection to the men who moved among them. Those stacks were only part of a shanty town, a fiercely rushed and noisy place with the sea on one side and on the other the staggered rise of tenement caves lurching oddly up the slope to a crest over which the Turks lobbed their shells.

Between sea and crest, business was carried on, the business of a grimly fighting army. Senior officers' quarters and administrative offices were down there, together with the wireless station which had been erected and the casualty clearing stations. A little way up the slope were the stacks of the water-condensing plant and near by two small compounds, one for Turkish prisoners, the other for pack-mules. The crash and racket of shellfire was added to by the clangour of a smithy beside the mule yard, and the smoke from that mingled with the blacker and smellier smoke of an incinerator and the pervasive odour of high explosive. There were men everywhere, laying lines from the telephone exchange, working in the bomb factory or the periscope factory — both open-air affairs — men moving purposefully, hesitantly, fearfully; men loitering, running, sitting and yarning; men bleeding and bandaged, straining under the weight of hand-hefted supplies; and men lying dead, draped and docketed and awaiting a barge and a burial. The English journalist Ellis Ashmead-Bartlett wrote of Anzac cove that it "reminded one irresistibly of a gigantic shipwreck. It looked as if the whole force and all the guns and material had not been landed but had been washed ashore."

If a man walked a kilometre or so in any direction away from that crowded beach he was in enemy territory. Wherever he was in that crescent he was under Turkish fire. He was "at the front" as soon as he landed, but at the front of "the front" he was often only a few metres from a Turkish strongpoint, nearer to the enemy than

The stack of a steam engine goes up at General Birdwood's field headquarters at Anzac Cove, while a boiler makes a temporary shelter. Officers as well as troops had to make shift with what they had.

to his own forces. Even in the shelters on the reverse slopes he was generally no more than 30 metres or so from the firing line. And there were a number of places where the Anzacs were, with determination, pushing closer all the time, places where open saps were dug through the rough soil in outgoing finger-like lines, groping forward till they were linked together by a crosscut which became a new forward trench line.

Other digging went on entirely below the ground. Men who had worked gold and coal in their civilian lives were recruited for that deeper digging, and they moled and beavered away by candlelight and naphtha flare, often barefoot, voices held to whispers as they picked and scraped gently and carefully towards Turkish emplacements and set explosives beneath them. The diggers working down in those places lost the look of sunlight and became pallid and often

enough trembled with the added tension of air-lessness and unsupported rock and the sudden shocking sound of Turkish picks close by where the enemy was doing the same killing work. Whatever the weather above ground, below was always a little chill, even the throat-choking dust seeming to strike cold and damp. Men with colds or mild infections sweated at the work and coughed and fell ill with influenza or bronchitis or worked on with itching skins and swollen eyes, trying desperately to hold back coughs and sneezes for fear the Turkish miners would hear them. There were places where they did more than hear, where the thin walls between sap and tunnel were breached, where bombs were 109

thrown and small mines exploded and the broken dead were dragged out of the reeking underground into the stinking air above.

Barricades would go up across those mole runs under the trenches, and they became basement battlegrounds where Turk and Anzac sometimes met with quiet ferocity, fighting hand to hand with bayonet and spade and pick in the dark belly of Gallipoli. Sergeant Cyril Lawrence of the Australian Engineers describes in his diary how, after a counter-mine had blown in part of the Australian diggings, he and his fellows, choking in gas and dust, reached the body of one of their mates "who had been driven right into the opposite wall of the tunnel and we had great difficulty in getting him out." A Victorian gunner described the awful business of burial of the dead when he wrote, "The bodies were that swollen and rotten that their clothes are bursting at the seams. We work with handkerchiefs around our noses and hook a couple of drag ropes around his ankles and drag him in and chop his arms in and fill up lively." Speed at filling in the hole was essential.

Below ground and above, on the beach and in the firing line, September was the month in which the movement slowed and the spark burned low. All the necessary things were done but at a reduced pace; no one seemed to have the energy or the desire; there had been too much killing in too short a time for too little purpose, and it seemed to have drained men of their powerful passions. On the Turkish side, Ramadan, a month-long period of daylight fasts, went by with no major attacks forthcoming. It was plain that the enemy was as tired and had been as badly bled as the Anzacs.

Water condensers and some of the bigger storage areas stand partly protected by the fold in the hills behind Anzac Cove.

In the closing days of September, Bulgaria mobilised her army and gave Germany passage to send arms and supplies through to Turkey. Greece and Serbia at once asked the Allies for protection for their eastern borders, and, however reluctantly, one British and one French division were withdrawn from Gallipoli for that purpose. With his forces so much depleted by that move, Hamilton wrote in his final dispatch to Lord Kitchener, "Sickness, the legacy of a desperately trying summer, took heavy toll of the survivors of so many arduous conflicts. No longer was there any question of operations on the grand scale."

Hamilton's own staff had by then realised that something more had to be done than their general was capable of doing. Their personal loyalty to and liking for him were unquestioned. But their professional, military feelings were that the time had come for some firm decisions to be made about Hamilton and his actions.

By the end of September, in London and in Australia, among politicians and soldiers, there was a wind of disquiet stirring, and casualty figures made for growing unease and a feeling that a firm decision had to be made about the Dardanelles before the potential political danger became a political and national disaster.

And on Gallipoli, the end of September brought the first of the chill nights, the first hint that the full blaze of summer was over. It was in those dying days that the Serbian border was crossed by German, Austrian and Bulgarian troops and the government of France urged

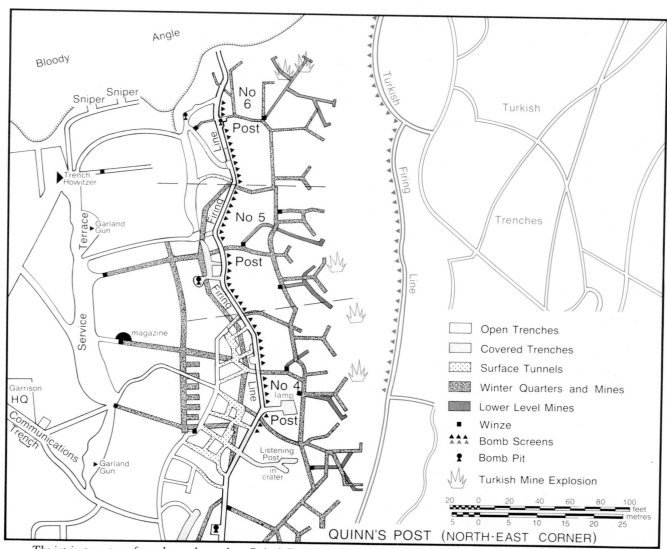

QUINN'S POST (NORTH-EAST CORNER)

Angle
Bloody
Sniper Sniper
Trench Howitzer
Terrace
Garland Gun
No 6 Post
No 5 Post
Firing Line
Firing Line
Service
magazine
Garrison HQ
Communications Trench
Garland Gun
No 4 Post
lamp
Listening Post in crater
Turkish Firing Line
Turkish Firing Trenches
Turkish

Open Trenches
Covered Trenches
Surface Tunnels
Winter Quarters and Mines
Lower Level Mines
■ Winze
▲▲▲ Bomb Screens
Bomb Pit
Turkish Mine Explosion

20 0   20   40   60   80 100
                            feet
5   0   5   10   15   20   25
                            metres

The intricate system of trenches and tunnels at Quinn's Post. At one point, Turkish and Anzac trenches were only 15 metres apart, and their tunnels intertwined.

immediate Allied support for Serbia even if that meant the evacuation of Gallipoli.

Almost six months after it began, the Dardanelles campaign was being openly spoken of as unwinnable. The first plain suggestion to evacuate the peninsula had been made more than a month earlier, on August 22, when it was clear that the Suvla Plan was not working. The pro-withdrawal forces had been building up support in the time since then, and October saw the outbreak of a different kind of warfare, as vicious and as deadly as any open fighting, although all it wounded and killed were reputations and policies.

General Stopford's overt attacks against Hamilton's actions and direction of the campaign were strong enough to override the fact that he had himself been relieved of command, and he was very well supported in his criticisms by growing numbers who disagreed with or were shocked by the handling of the Gallipoli operation. Even for the people of a Britain which was becoming inured to hideous losses on the Western Front, the casualty lists from the comparatively small Dardanelles theatre were traumatic. For the distant underpopulated lands of Australia and New Zealand, the Anzac casualties were appalling, and there was a swell of opinion against the Dardanelles, against the war, even, to some extent, a resurgence of the anti-British feeling that had hung on after the Boer War.

The move to withdraw from Gallipoli was nevertheless resisted on both sides of the world, perhaps less from a belief in any ultimate success than from a desire to put off the inevitable and its equally inevitable political and military consequences. Indeed, In Australia, Prime Minister William Morris Hughes, who had succeeded Andrew Fisher, was prepared to offer Great Britain another army corps of 50,000 men – without necessarily considering whether there would be that many volunteers. When a storm of criticism began to build because of his offer, Hughes summed up his and his supporters' side of the argument: "We have no responsibility in directing the campaign. Our business is only to carry out the instructions of the Imperial Government. We must give all the assistance we can, and at all events we owe the Imperial Government this duty – refraining from criticising any position of vital responsibility."

But despite Hughes's unequivocal and unquestioning support, the winds of criticism were rising. Most of the anger was directed towards the man who held a "position of vital responsibility" – General Sir Ian Hamilton. There was a confluence of events, the sort of coming together in one short period of a number of diverse things, all of which, combined, go on to shape a new pattern. Ellis Ashmead-Bartlett and the Australian journalist Keith Murdoch had sent critical reports to their respective prime ministers on the conduct of the Dardanelles campaign at a time when confidence in Hamilton and the operations he commanded was sagging. Now a member of the Commander-in-Chief's own staff, Major Guy Dawnay, sent to London by Hamilton to report to Kitchener, was commenting unfavourably on his chief, not out of disloyalty but out of concern.

On October 11, Kitchener sent Hamilton a signal asking for his estimate of the losses that would be involved in an evacuation of the peninsula. Hamilton signalled back his belief that evacuation could lead to losses as high as 50 per cent and that to him such a step was unthinkable. It was that reply which was tabled before the Dardanelles Committee on October 14 after a night during which there had been a heavy zeppelin raid on London. The largely sleepless members of the committee, never likely to get along smoothly, fought a short, sharp battle – Churchill, still fiercely in favour of the Dardanelles campaign, losing to the majority. Kitchener was required by the committee to tell Hamilton of their decision, and on October 16 he sent the signal recalling Hamilton to London, where he was informed that the government "desired a fresh, unbiased opinion, from a responsible commander, upon the question of early evacuation."

The responsible commander appointed in Hamilton's place was General Sir Charles

A BROADSIDE FROM THE PRESS

Journalist Keith Murdoch on his visit to Gallipoli in August 1915. Right: C. E. W. Bean, Australia's official war correspondent, rides ahead of the English journalist Ellis Ashmead-Bartlett during a horseback excursion on the island of Imbros, where the war correspondents were based.

People in the south of England could hear the guns roaring in France. The war was there, on their doorstep, and the flow of wounded and men on leave came to them direct. No one came from Gallipoli in the murderous months of that campaign, and at the outset there was almost no news from the Dardanelles.

The officially accredited journalists on Gallipoli were kept to a handful. There was an anonymous "man from Reuter's", who seems to have filed virtually no stories at all; Henry Nevinson and Ellis Ashmead-Bartlett represented the British press; and C.E.W. Bean was appointed official observer for the Australian government. All of them – and the occasional journalist given permission to visit – had to sign an agreement to submit stories to the military censor, who would allow no criticism of the conduct of the campaign.

As the months wore away, however, rumours began seeping back to London that there was great discontent at Gallipoli and near-total distrust of the command and staff there for their mismanagement of the campaign. Much of that feeling was expressed by Ashmead-Bartlett,

who had been from the first a constant critic of Hamilton's strategy and lesser commanders' tactics. In mid-September he found a way to bypass the censor.

A young Australian journalist, Keith Murdoch, was on his way to England and had been given permission by Hamilton to visit Anzac. Murdoch, strong-minded and fiercely nationalistic, was appalled at the conditions and the attitudes he found there. Ashmead-Bartlett saw in the young Australian the prospect of getting his story out; he briefed Murdoch carefully and gave him a letter to be handed to Prime Minister Herbert Asquith.

At Marseilles, on his way to London, Murdoch was arrested by a British officer supported by French police and not freed until he handed over Ashmead-Bartlett's letter. Years later it was revealed that their fellow-correspondent, Henry Nevinson, had overheard the plan and had informed Hamilton of it; Hamilton in turn had arranged that Murdoch should be stopped.

Murdoch was unstoppable, however, in another, more important, sense. The very fact that the British had taken Ashmead-Bartlett's

letter from him made him more determined that the story should be told, and neither his very brief stay at Anzac nor his inexperience prevented him from writing his own letter – an impassioned 8,000 words to Prime Minister Andrew Fisher of Australia. His highly coloured prose was a combination of Ashmead-Bartlett's opinions and his own reactions to what he had seen.

Murdoch met almost every member of the cabinet in London. His passion was hard to resist and most notably affected Lloyd George, who passed a copy of the Murdoch letter to Asquith. From Asquith's office it was printed and circulated to the Imperial Defence Committee and to the Dardanelles Committee as an official state paper.

Ashmead-Bartlett was sent back to England, where he and Murdoch were supported by Lord Northcliffe, whose newspapers gave the widest coverage to their stories. There can be no doubt that the information and opinions expressed by Murdoch and Ashmead-Bartlett carried very considerable weight in both the recall of Hamilton and in the withdrawal from Gallipoli. The pen had indeed outweighed the sword.

Monro, who was at that time commanding the First Army in Flanders. Until Monro's arrival, Birdwood was placed temporarily in charge, and he sent a farewell message to Hamilton on behalf of his men. It said: "Anzac greatly regrets your departure and, in wishing you goodbye, all ranks offer you personally their very best wishes." While there is no doubt that Hamilton was a charming, intelligent and likeable man, it is hard to see many of the troops on Gallipoli agreeing with Birdwood's expressed sentiments.

They, the fighting men, had suffered and were suffering a physical degeneration which was rapidly being matched by the mental slowing and weakening the awful months had forced on them. The useless savagery of August had been a blow from which the survivors did not recover in anything like full measure, so that now, weeks of continued fighting later, they crouched, smeared with dirt and clay, bearded and foul, sunken-cheeked and hollow-eyed, weary to their bones and most of them ill. Around them was plain horror. The war correspondent Henry Nevinson wrote, "The dead were lying about in great numbers; the hands and faces of hastily buried men protruded from the ground, and as I walked I felt at intervals the squelching softness of a man's body, scarcely covered beneath the soil."

The October days still held some heat, and there was still fighting to be done, no matter how hard it was for men to move and to concentrate on the desperate needs of close combat. The flies were still there, feasting on the blackened and swolled dead, untouched by the shrapnel and bullets which went on killing men. The wounded were still being racked and jolted laboriously down the gullies and tracks to increasingly congested aid stations. Water was still scarce; sometimes it was impossible to move any water at all forward to posts where shaky men clung to firing points which were little more than scratches on the face of the land. And always, it seemed, there was Turkish fire falling on them from above.

Many of the men were suffering from forms of trench foot, evil-smelling fungus growths between the toes; many of them also had got mates to rough-cut their hair back close to the scalp as a measure of louse control. Almost every man was underweight, and no one was free of the edginess and nerves engendered by the living conditions, the poor food and the constant, unremitting danger.

When General Monro arrived, on October 28, he began his task with meetings and brisk discussions with his new staff. Monro was a professional soldier, pragmatic, firm-minded and not particularly imaginative. He asked simple and straightforward questions: Could the Turkish positions be taken by the forces on the peninsula, and could the Allied troops hold out through the coming winter? The staff responses to his questions were scarcely optimistic. They boiled down to the expressed belief that the troops might be able to sustain a single 24-hour attack but that if they were counter-attacked "they could only do their best". The men were not equipped for winter weather, let alone a winter offensive; no unit was at its proper strength, and their supporting artillery was rationed to two shells a day for each gun.

It hardly needed the depressed statements of the Gallipoli officers to convince Monro. Even coming as he did from the mud-and-blood awfulness of the Flanders front, what he saw at Gallipoli was a great and immediate shock. The men who had been clinging on there for months had become accustomed to the conditions, to the way they looked and lived, to the ramshackle, junk-heap appearance of everything and the dung-pile stink; Monro came to it with fresh eyes and saw it for what it was – a disaster. But his immediate signal to Kitchener said nothing about evacuation, giving only his first impressions and asking for supplies of winter material to be sent out. His instructions had stipulated that he report "on purely military grounds" whether it was better to evacuate Gallipoli or to try again to take the peninsula. Further, he had been told to estimate the likely loss in evacuation as against the number of troops needed to conclude the campaign successfully. When he made no specific recommendations in

General Hamilton (right) stands with Admiral John de Robeck on board HMS Triad on the afternoon of Hamilton's departure for England after his recall.

General Sir Ian Hamilton, commander of the Mediterranean Expeditionary Force.

THE SWORD-AND-PEN GENERAL

General Sir Ian Hamilton was much of the old Elizabethan poet–soldier, the rounded man, to whom letters and the sword were balancing sides of the one nature. He was a lifelong diary keeper, making his copious and detailed entries in French, many of them forming bases for published works such as *The Fighting of the Future* .

Born on the Mediterranean island of Corfu in 1853 – the year in which the Crimean War began – Hamilton was a professional soldier from his adolescence, amassing more military experience than almost any other general in the British army. He was also a man of great charm, who drew people to him in friendship.

It has become easy and fashionable to deride Hamilton's actions in command at Gallipoli, to accuse him of distancing himself from the fighting, of being unrealistic in his demands and wantonly extravagant with the lives of his men. Yet he was largely exonerated by the Dardanelles Commission in its report published after the war.

Whatever was said about him, it was undoubted that he had been recommended for the Victoria Cross three times, that he suffered from a shattered left hand and a brutally set leg, that he was a brave and charming man, and while his post-war book, *Gallipoli Diary*, did nothing to endear him to his detractors, it is equally true that nothing marred his general popularity.

After leaving the army, he served as Lieutenant of the Tower of London and later was elected Rector of Edinburgh University. A picture of him as an old man shows a slim and elegant figure, a hawk nose over a bristle of white moustache and the mouth curled in a smile – perhaps because he had outlived all his old opponents. He saw the whole of World War II and was 94 years old when he died in 1947. A third of his life had been lived after the deathroll closed at Gallipoli.

By the time General Monro arrived at Gallipoli to take over from General Hamilton, Anzac Cove had the appearance of a junk-heap with humpy-like structures (above) and manned by bedraggled caretakers. At left, two soldiers in winter clothes watch over stacks of bully beef cases.

Brigade headquarters of the 4th Australian Infantry Brigade, below Sari Bair.

that first signal, Kitchener impatiently cabled to him, "Please send me as soon as possible your report on the main issue at the Dardanelles, namely, leaving or staying." On October 30 Monro started a sweeping tour of Cape Helles, Anzac and Suvla and two days later recommended evacuation.

While Monro had been at Gallipoli, one of the Dardanelles naval officers had been heading for London. Commodore Roger Keyes, acting against his admiral's beliefs, went to Arthur Balfour, the First Lord of the Admiralty, and to the Chief of War Staff, Admiral Oliver, and began to preach the gospel of a renewed attack, a combined navy-and-army attack, ships bursting through the Narrows in parallel with gunboats on the Aegean coast, both fleets acting in concert with soldiers to clip the peninsula at Bulair and then storm out and into Turkey's European mainland and the Sea of Marmara. At a time when the prevailing mood in London was one of acute depression and pessimism about the Dardanelles, Keyes's fiery approach was both startling and, to many, invigorating.

Kitchener had been shocked by Monro's recommendation, and he seized on Keyes's plan as a possible way out of the whole Gallipoli problem. Balfour agreed that the navy could well push an attack, provided the army meant business. Once again the inter-service rivalries became apparent, and although the senior officers of both arms appeared to share similar views about a proposed operation, a confidential report stated bluntly, "One must not be led by the mutual expressions of confidence, admiration and eulogy to think that on no occasion was there any impatience or criticism of the methods or work of the other arm." Keyes, though, was single-minded in his advocacy of a combined assault. He had believed – and said openly – since March that the navy had let the soldiers down, and he pushed hard for an attack in which his own arm would play its proper part. His fervour as much as anything swayed Kitchener's opinion.

No matter that, in the field, conditions were still ghastly, that in the fire-pits and entrenchments and on the bare and raddled patches of ground between the lines, men were still digging and crawling and struggling and dying. No matter that the heat was going out of the days at this fag end of October and that the nights were now cold and becoming colder – and that winter supplies had not been sent. None of those things seemed to matter as much as Keyes's fire combined with Kitchener's abhorence of the idea of withdrawal. Monro's recommendation to evacuate Gallipoli was rejected.

"Australia will stand behind the
Mother Country...to our last
man and our last shilling"

Waiting for news from Gallipoli outside the offices of the Melbourne Argus.

Registered at the General Post Office, Sydney, for transmission by Post as a Newspaper.　　　No. 170; Vol. VII. (New Series).—No. 2629; Vol. XCIII. (Old Series)

THE
SYNDEY **Mail**
=PRICE=
THREEPENCE

AN AUSTRALIAN WEEKLY　　| June 30, 1915.

WAR ISSUE—No. XLVIII.

A PATRIOTIC FERVOUR

In the tide of fervour that washed over Australia with the outbreak of the Great War, there was a huge wave of patriotism. It was not so much for Australia as for the Empire, epitomised by the Crown and the Mother Country. Prime Minister Andrew Fisher had expressed popular feeling when he promised, "Australia will stand behind the Mother Country to help and defend her to our last man and our last shilling."

Remote from the sound of guns or the sight of hospital ships and trains, the population of Australia seemed to be an amalgam of volunteers training for action, adolescents waiting to enlist, and women, children and oldsters all performing some service. There was work to be had in war-related industries, work for women to do so that men could be released to fight. There were good deeds to be done—collecting for and packing "comfort" parcels to send to the troops overseas; organising theatricals and tableaux to raise money for those parcels; learning first aid to help the wounded and the sick.

It was the casualty lists that brought the war home. No banner headlines shouting of great victories could outweigh the growing columns of names of those who would not come back or who would come back maimed. The small photographs of the dead were more influential than editorials or reports of politicians' statements. Within three weeks of the landing at Gallipoli, just under 500 casualties had been named to the public; within two months of the landing, the figure had risen close to 10,000—and every day's newspapers carried more.

Capt. C. E. Leer,
3rd Batt., N.S.W.—Killed.

Capt. R. Burns,
3rd Batt., N.S.W.—Killed.

HEROES OF THE DARDANELLES.

*L*AST week we published portraits of nearly 100 of our Australian Soldiers who have been killed or wounded at the Dardanelles. Many more are reproduced in this issue, several additional casualty lists having been made available during the week.

Lieut. R. O. Cowey,
3rd Batt., N.S.W.—Wounded.

Lieut. P. S. S. Woodforde,
1st Batt., N.S.W.—Wounded.

Capt. J. F. Walsh,
15th Batt., Qld.—Killed.

Lieut. T. Robertson,
15th Batt., Qld.—Wounded.

Lieut. G. Thomas,
9th Batt., Qld.—Killed.

Lieut. J. W. Costin,
9th Batt., Qld.—Killed.

Lieut. F. G. Hayman,
9th Batt., Qld.—Killed.

Corpl. H. F. Paton,
9th Batt., Qld.—Wounded.

Sgt. A. P. H. Adair,
9th Batt., Qld.—Wounded.

Pte. J. R. Spreadborough,
9th Batt., Qld.—Wounded.

Pte. A. D. Mitchell,
1st Batt., N.S.W.—Died of Wounds.

Lce.-Corpl. A. A. Anderson,
1st Batt., N.S.W.—Wounded.

Pte. F. J. Bayliss,
2nd Batt., N.S.W.—Wounded.

Sap. F. R. Cluett,
1st Field Coy. Eng., N.S.W.—Wounded.

Pte. H. E. Smith,
13th Batt., N.S.W.—Wounded.

Pte. H. R. Cross,
2nd Batt., N.S.W.—Wounded.

Sap. L. G. F. Burton,
1st Field Co. Eng., N.S.W.—Wounded.

Pte. P. Smith,
14th Batt., Vic.—Died of Wounds.

Pte. G. L. Thompson,
5th Batt., Vic.—Killed.

Pte. B. J. Young,
5th Batt., Vic.—Wounded.

Pte. E. H. Cheal,
3rd Batt., N.S.W.—Died of Wounds.

Pte. F. T. Wright,
2nd Batt., N.S.W.—Died of Wounds.

123

ENTHUSIASM WANES

Although patriotic postcards abounded and an outward show of support for the war continued, the fervent patriotism that had first swept Australia soon began to flag. The casualty rates were too grim, and they affected too many homes across the continent. Everyone suffered or was close to a sufferer.

Enlistment figures dropped significantly. In response, new pressures were applied – street-corner recruiters, films, even urgings from pulpits. By the middle of 1915, height, weight, age and other physical requirements were reduced in order to make more men eligible for military service. It did little to improve recruitment figures. Small bands of volunteers marched up to 500 kilometres from bush towns to Sydney, recruiting as they went, but their success was small.

Anzac Day Memorial.

HE'LL BE HOME SOON.
SICK AND WOUNDED.

GIVE HIM A HELPING HAND.

AUSTRALIAN NATIONAL ANTHEM.

God bless Australia's Sons
Fighting courageously,
  God guide our Sons.
Help them to live and die
Glorious in victory,
Comfort all those who sigh,
  God save our Sons.

Protect our gallant sons!
Nobly defending us
  On alien shores;
Give us strong faith in Thee,
Our sons again to see,
Loud shall our praises be,
  God save them all.

Part of our Nation grand,
Loyal as one we stand,
  God bless us all.
Strong make us in the fight
'Gainst wrong, and for the right,
Our hope in Thee is bright,
  God save us all.

God cause all wars to cease,
Send us a righteous peace,
  On Thee we call;
Help us all sin to shun,
May Thine own will be done,
The world for Christ be won,
  God save us all.

COPYRIGHT.   SPES IN DEO.

The "Coo-ees" arrive at Martin Place, Sydney on November 12, 1915, at the end of a 512-kilometre recruiting march from Gilgandra, NSW. Volunteers joined in all along the route.

Fancy Costumes at "The Girls They Left Behind" Ball at Masonic Hall, Oct. 23

This is the second dance organised by these girls and held in aid of Wounded Soldiers Rest Home at Wirths' Park.

(1) Misses Mitchell and Rodway, Dutch Couple. (2) Miss Cameron, Pierrot. (3) Miss Hilda O'Meara, Futurist Pierrot. (4) Miss McCallister, John Bull. (5) Misses Montgomery and Craig, Dutch Couple. (6) Miss Davidson, Simple Simon. (7) Committee (standing): Misses E. McLeod, J. Watson, E. Gibbons, J. Willis, M. Hepburn, M. Bailey, D. Jones, F. Livingstone; (sitting): M. Kewley, E. Blemeres, N. Millar (hon. sec.), E. Roberts (hon. treas.), M. Shrimpton. Sitting in front: M. Setford and E. Hill. (8) Miss Ivie Driscoll, Mabel from the Keystone Pictures. (9) Miss Lyons, The Monk and the Org. (10) Miss L. Tregligas, Early Victorian. (11) Misses Eva Kendall and Blanche Kidd, Harem Ladies. (12) Misses Scott and Murray, Buster Brown.... S. R. Shier, Photo.

126

Dulcie Davenport, aged 2 years,
Who collected over £4 for our wounded soldiers.

DOING THEIR BIT

Women and children found many ways to raise funds for the war effort and make "comforts" for the troops — although such activities as the fancy-dress dance reported in *Table Talk* *(opposite)* may not have given much comfort to a soldier reading about it in his trench on Gallipoli. It was common for children to be dressed up in miniature uniform or patriotic regalia like little Dulcie Davenport *(left)* to collect pennies from passers-by for "our brave boys at the front". And schoolboys even took to knitting and sewing. The picture below shows pupils of Byron Bay (NSW) Public School "making articles of various kinds for the use of our soldiers," as the *Sydney Mail* reported, adding, "The boys are as enthusiastic as the girls."

THE BOYS PROUDLY DO THEIR PART.

FROM THUNDER OF CANNON TO MUSIC OF SYDNEY.

AN AUSTRALIAN NURSE AND SOME OF HER CHARGES.
A snapshot as the steamer Ballarat, conveying the sick and wounded soldiers, drew up to the wharf in Woolloomooloo Bay.

SMILES AND CIGARETTES FOR BRAVE MEN.
The public has a sensitive conscience regarding what is due to the returned soldiers, and there are many willing workers to assist in assuring the brave volunteers that their names and achievements are dear to their fellow-citizens. Our picture shows that the work—a labour of love—gives happiness on both sides.

THE RED CROSS

There are some universal symbols of peace and comfort—the dove, the palm leaf and, for men at war, the Red Cross. Beneath the symbol which had begun as a Crusaders' emblem, women of all kinds volunteered to work, often in appalling conditions, to ease the pain and sometimes the last hours of wounded Anzacs. Some of them may have realised that the enemy's wounds were being tended by veiled women wearing the Red Crescent on their uniforms.

At home in Australia, Red Cross workers helped to comfort and restore to health wounded soldiers in hospitals and convalescent homes. They arranged outings and diversions, read to incapacitated soldiers, or just provided company or a sympathetic ear. Meanwhile, they were still busy knitting, sewing and collecting for the troops still at the front.

THE SYDNEY **MAIL**

Wednesday, August 18, 1915.

Back Home !

IN this interesting photograph we see one of the wounded heroes of Gallipoli relating his experiences abroad to a Red Cross worker, whose fingers, as she listens, are deftly knitting for a soldier at the front. The picture was taken on the occasion of a launch picnic to convalescent soldiers who are installed in a cottage at Cronulla, kindly placed at the disposal of the Red Cross Society by Miss Piper, who is seen in the photograph standing.

WELCOMING OUR WOUNDED HEROES HOME.

News photographs show the mixture of joy and anxiety on the faces of the crowds at the wharves to greet the Anzac wounded returning from Gallipoli. Six months after the landings, the casualty lists in the papers suddenly became maimed, blinded and limping men. And there were too many of them not coming back at all.

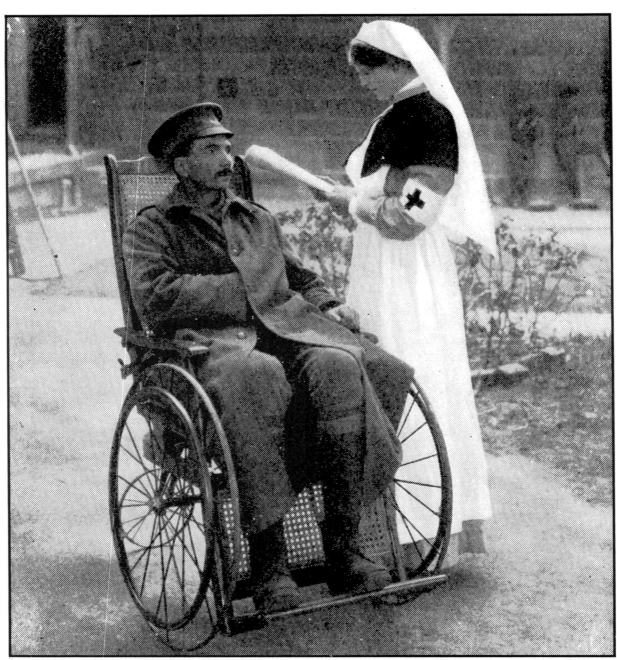

At No. 4 General Hospital, Randwick, in Sydney, a nurse reads the latest war news to a soldier recently returned from Gallipoli.

PORTRAITS FOUND ON THE BATTLEFIELDS OF ANZAC.

THESE portraits were handed to the "Mail" by Private R. Benson, of the 4th Battalion, who recently returned to Sydney. He was wounded on two occasions, and in all received 16 distinct wounds—chiefly from hand-grenades. The photographs were found after heavy fighting in the early part of the campaign—the first in the row on May 1, the second on April 30, the third on May 2, and the fourth on May 6. Private Benson is anxious to return them to those who have a claim to them. His address is the Soldiers' Club, George-street, Sydney.

6

THE WICKED WIND OF WINTER

Withdrawal from Gallipoli was now being recommended. But first the Anzacs had to withstand the assault of a new enemy, the bitter winter weather. It eased, fortunately, to coincide with the successful evacuation of 85,000 Allied troops.

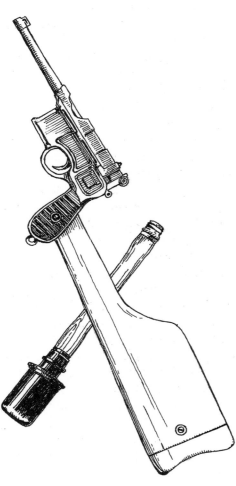

Mauser 9 mm automatic pistol with a wooden holster which converted into a shoulder stock. Behind the stock is a stick grenade.

Monro's recommendation was the sober and well-considered work of a seasoned soldier. It said bluntly that any renewed offensive would bring losses of 30 to 40 per cent in men and matériel, and in that estimate he was supported by the senior men on the spot, those who could be expected to know best. Monro, thorough and professional, drew up a draft plan for evacuation of the peninsula and then left for Egypt to confer with General Sir John Maxwell, the Commander-in-Chief there, about the details of such a withdrawal. He gave Birdwood the temporary command.

On November 3, Birdwood was awakened by a signal from Kitchener which staggered him: "Most secret. Decipher yourself. Tell no one. You know Monro's report. I leave here tomorrow night to come out to you. Have seen Keyes and the Admiralty will, I believe, agree naval attempt to force straits. We must do what we can to assist them, and I think as soon as ships are in the Marmara we should seize and hold the isthmus so as to supply them if Turks hold out. Examine very carefully best position for landing near marsh at head of Gulf of Xeros, so that we could get a line across at isthmus with ships on both sides. To find troops for this purpose we should have to reduce to lowest possible numbers the men in all the trenches, and perhaps evacuate positions at Suvla. All the best fighting men that could be spared, including your boys from Anzac reinforcements I can sweep up in Egypt, might be concentrated at Mudros ready for this enterprise. We must do it right this time. I absolutely refuse to sign order for evacuation, which I think would be the greatest disaster and would condemn a large percentage of our men to death or imprisonment. Monro will be appointed to command the Salonika force."

So by November 4, within a week of his appointment, Monro had lost the Gallipoli command and been relegated to the more-or-less standby force at Salonika, and Birdwood was formally advised that he was now in command of the Dardanelles campaign. And, although Birdwood was not then aware of it, on that same day Keyes got the fleet reinforcements he had suggested would be needed for forcing the Narrows. There was no way he could know, either, that Kitchener was preparing to leave for an examination of Gallipoli because he was being sent there by Prime Minister Asquith, who was being assailed in his coalition cabinet by Lloyd George and Bonar Law in favour of pulling out of the Dardanelles.

In the Parliament the schisms widened and deepened between the Easterners and the Westerners, and those gaps cut across traditional party lines; political futures were jeopardised, and ministers and members were threatening to resign over the issue. All that, plus the fact that Kitchener's reputation had suffered badly because of the events since April, gave Asquith the chance to get his Secretary of State for War out of the way for a while, with instructions to report on the situation there himself. Asquith sent Lloyd George a note in which he said, "We avoid by this method of procedure the supercession of K as War Minister while achieving the same result."

In any case, Kitchener's sense of responsibility made him feel duty bound to see for himself what was happening to the men in his charge.

He said to Asquith, "I pace my room at night and see the boats fired at and capsizing, and the drowning men. Perhaps if I have to lose a lot of men over there I shall not want to come back." A "lot of men" had already been lost.

Kitchener left London in a most uncertain mood, not sure which way his political masters might jump, not sure in his own mind—and that must have been a rare occurrence—whether the joint operation would, or could, go ahead. He had asked Keyes to meet him at Marseilles, but that belligerent sailor did not get the message. Someone at the Admiralty made the assumption that Keyes could never reach Marseilles in time, and the message was scrapped. Kitchener went on to Gallipoli for a three-day tour of inspection, a front-line visit; to the troops it was almost unbelievable that a British officer, the most senior one at that, should be so close to the dangers they had endured.

At that stage there were four possibilities being considered—the diversion of major efforts to Salonika in an attempt to assist Greece against Germany and her allies; a diversionary attack at Ayas Bay in Asiatic Turkey to cover a withdrawal from Gallipoli; a renewed naval-land attack on the Keyes pattern; and a straightforward withdrawal from the peninsula. The French, pushing for greater Allied intervention at Salonika, derided the Ayas Bay suggestion, and the British General Staff rejected it—but the same staff were also against any increased effort at Salonika. As for a new land-sea assault, there was no one in its favour except, perhaps, Keyes.

By the time Kitchener had spent three days looking at conditions at Gallipoli, at the state of the troops and the positions of the Turks, the issue was hardly in doubt. He telegraphed to London on November 15 advising that he felt that the cost in men of an evacuation could be far less than was originally estimated. It was not exactly a committed statement, and a week later the planning staff advisory committee informed Kitchener that the diversion at Ayas Bay was not considered, that Salonika would received two divisions as reinforcements—and that an answer was required of Kitchener: Did he 135 or did he not recommend evacuation?

On November 22 Lord Kitchener, first soldier of the realm, offered his reluctant opinion that a withdrawal should be made from Suvla and Anzac but that Cape Helles should be held for the time being. Despite that final, definitive response, it was more than two weeks before the formal orders were passed down. Monro, suddenly restored to favour, was given command of all eastern Mediterranean forces; within that overall command, Birdwood was to be in charge of the force at Gallipoli.

In London, while Kitchener was away, there was a shifting of political fortunes. The Dardanelles Committee was disbanded and replaced by the War Committee, giving Asquith the chance to get rid of some members. Among them was Winston Churchill, the man who had fought so hard and so long for the realisation of the dream of the Dardanelles – and who, for the rest of his life, would carry its failure like a stigma. Churchill resigned his seat and went back into the army in which he had started his adult life and which he had left as a young acting captain. He served in France, first as a major in the Grenadier Guards, then as a lieutenant-colonel commanding a battalion of the Royal Scots Fusiliers.

While the cross-currents of politics and policies swirled and eddied during the first half of November and before the firm word was passed about a withdrawal, the men of Anzac were increasingly aware of that prospect. In his brief spell in command, Monro, recognising the likelihood of evacuation and believing it to be the only proper course, ordered the setting-up of an initial plan for such a move. That plan had gone ahead in first-draft form, and there had even been a tentative start made on reducing some of the stockpiles of stores and ammunition. In an area as restricted as Anzac, it was impossible to keep anything as important as that a secret, and the strong impression quickly formed among the troops that there was an end in sight to the torment of the place they were in. It had 136 some oddly counterpoised results. The increas-

ingly open feeling that they were going to pull out meant that there developed a new kind of caution, a growing reluctance to take any kind of risk now that the ordeal was nearly over. There was a greater willingness to report sick, a feeling that it would not smack so much of deserting their mates if all of them were to get out anyway. Conversely, there grew a strange and sudden feeling of renewed strength, of a last desperate need to prove themselves, to maintain their standing in their own eyes, at least, as being undefeated, even if they had not been able to do what had been expected of them.

So, with a plan – not yet officially required – taking shape on paper, the men of Anzac kept their "normal" life going. Except that now the

a spell on the land. Since August there had been some stong winds, some rain, some storm squalls. Now and then it had been difficult to bring small boats inshore, and sometimes there had been a capsize, but the first half of November had been a blaze of splendid weather, an Indian summer of placid and surprising warmth. But then, with the swing of the month, wild winds began to blow from the south-west, and there was damage along the shoreline with lighters and small boats splintering along the beach and decking stripped from Watson's Pier by the rising seas and winds.

Under the provisional plan for withdrawal, the water-pumping station which had been built at one end of the beach had been partially dismantled. Now, under the heavy thrusts of the wind, the tall condensers and the piping were at risk of breaking—a serious consideration because it was becoming impossible for water barges and lighters to come in to the piers and jetties to unload their cargoes. Ironically, with heavy rain imminent, the prospect of thirst became a menace to the fighting men. For the fighting raged on, and the artillery went on smashing shrapnel into the Anzac positions, while the weather enemy built towards an unexpected and fearsome offensive.

By then the Allied forces stretched from the Asiatic side of the straits all the way up to Suvla Bay, north of Anzac. In those forces were men from Australia and New Zealand and Britain, from France and India and Nepal and Africa; there were labour battalions and corps of Greeks and Egyptians, Maltese and Palestinians. Many of those men, soldiers and labourers alike, had experience of winter climates, but many thousands of them had never experienced truly cold weather or the sting of freezing rain or the bite of ice, and very little provision had been made for their protection. Monro's request for winter clothing had presumably been lost

extra tasks involved in preparing to pull out were added to the fighting and the fatigues. And while the staff planned major deception strategies, the troops worked out personal ways to fool the enemy. Meantime, stretcher-bearers were still working their ragged ways down the slopes with wounded; groups out of the immediate front line were still hauling and man-handling and digging, still carting water up to forward positons; the few men of the Light Horse who were still mounted for their work as dispatch-riders were still galloping at full tilt along the beach under sniper fire, and their mates were still taking bets on whether or not they would make the distance without being hit.

The November weather seemed to have laid

Seas whipped up by November's violent winds batter Watson's Pier. Installations were smashed and boats wrecked during the storm.

in the shuffle of indecision which had marked a good deal of November. Most of the fighting men in all three areas — Helles, Anzac and Suvla — had been issued with mackintosh capes or groundsheets; many of them had been given rubber boots, and there was a small issue of rum; but taken in all it was scarcely a sufficient safeguard. Yet the weather and its threat seemed for a short time less important, less nerve-racking, than the oddly silent three days from November 24 to 27.

One of the factors about a withdrawal which had been discussed by the planners was the silence from the Anzac lines; a drop in noise level would be bound to alert the Turks. A possible solution to the problem lay in accustoming the enemy to spells of greatly reduced noise and activity so that the real thing would not come as an alarm to them. As a consequence, the "silent stunt" was devised. The order went out that for a fixed period there was to be none of the usual firing or artillery tasks; the enemy was to be shot at only if he attacked or showed clear signs of attacking. For three days, then, the Anzacs suffered a new, a different and near-intolerable strain — facing an increasingly perplexed enemy who still bombed and patrolled and fired as aggressively as always, yet forbidden to fire back at them unless he overtly attacked. The leash was to restrain the Anzacs till midnight on November 27.

As it drew towards that hour, the other enemy struck. Bitterly cold rain began to fall, first as a thin and chill drizzle, then as a downpour and then lashing and whipping the troops as it rode on a howling wind from the north-east. As the "silent stunt" ended and the day turned over, the rain became sleet and then snow, and for two full days and nights the freezing wind swept the peninsula, carrying flurries of snow and great torrents of icy rain. Frozen snow lay on the hillsides and the low branches of the twisted little trees; there were icicles hanging in the trenches; rifles and machine-guns jammed and soaked men coughed and shivered in their trenches.

At the height of the awfulness, rain water rushed and welled down the abrupt slopes and gullies, swamping trenches and shelters, drowning men and mules, washing out some positions entirely, sweeping down drowned

Turkish and Anzac soldiers alike and mixing the newly dead with the remains of hidden or shallow-buried corpses of both sides. Men leaped and floundered away from water-filled and collapsing trenches, and, from above, Turks in more secure positions opened a heavy fire – although before long that died away under the cold hammers of the wind and rain.

Dawn and then watery daylight brought no relief. November 28 was long known among British soldiers as "Frozen Foot Day"; John Masefield refers to it as "a day more terrible than any battle" and suggests, probably with justice, that either side could have taken the other's position if there had been enough unfrosted feet for an advance. At the shoreline, piers and jetties were destroyed or badly damaged, and the wreckage of boats lay everywhere. Water-pipes had frozen and burst, and the turmoil of wet and icy winds had tossed stores about with abandon and pulled down shelters.

Men who had never seen snow in their lives froze to death in their trenches, and men who had been brought up in cold northern climates died or were frostbitten for lack of protective clothing. While the incidence of fly-borne disease dropped sharply and immediately, other kinds of casualties mounted frighteningly. In the week after that savage and arctic battering, more than 15,000 men were evacuated suffering from exposure, frostbite, trench foot and bronchial ailments. More than 200 died on Anzac from the bite of the wind alone.

General Monro, as commander in the eastern Mediterranean, and Birdwood, commanding on Gallipoli, both saw at once how this precursor of a possibly more severe winter placed an enormous new danger in the path of successful evacuation and how any delay could lead to total disaster. Monro telegraphed London urgently for decisive orders.

Kitchener was travelling home by way of a conference on the island of Lemnos to determine what level of help – if any – should be given at Salonika and how the Gallipoli front might be affected. He was unequivocal in his report to the War Committee, writing that "the evacuation of Suvla and Anzac should be proceeded with. Cape Helles could be held for the present."

Admiral Lord Rosslyn Wemyss, acting for Admiral de Robeck, protested strongly. He asked for one more effort at a concerted land-sea assault, and his argument was sufficiently pursuasive to lead the War Committee and cabinet to reconsider such a possibility. Kitchener signalled to Monro to ask if the use of four extra divisions from Salonika plus a strong naval strike would swing the balance of Gallipoli so that it could, at least, be held during the winter months. Monro, realistic as always and supported by Birdwood, replied that such moves would result in no more than a minor advance, perhaps a few hundred metres. On December 5 an Allied Council met at Calais to discuss the Salonika-Dardanelles situation and reached no decision, but the next day the British and French military staffs met and were unanimous in their decision to defend Salonika, so committing the Allies to keeping a large and useful force locked away from the major fighting fronts for the rest of the war. Their decision included the complete evacuation of the Dardanelles.

There were men still at Anzac who had landed there on that first morning, April 25. There had been replacements and reinforcements, and they had watched as those raw troops – those who survived – took on the wasted and hollow-eyed look of Gallipoli veterans. They had thirsted and sickened, dried out and lost weight, been shot at all day and every day and listened night after night to the pitiful sounds of the wounded and the dying. Now, after seven anguished months, they were reduced to sucking dirty snow, still no closer to the campaign's objective – and they were still being shot at.

They had nearly a month yet to endure in that ghastly place. The decisive order did not come until the night of December 7–8, and Monro's foresight in starting an evacuation plan and preparation early proved to be of immense value. By the time the formal word came down, there was a good understanding of what things needed to be done, there was a rough schedule

Soldiers rug up as best they can against the bitter cold weather on "Frozen Foot Day", November 28.

Snow blankets the hillside down to the beach during the cold spell in November. Many men who had survived the enemy's bullets died from the cold.

for doing them, and there was the basis of an operational staff to see them properly done.

The solid structure of the plan was the combined work of an English officer – and the staff historian – Colonel C.F. Aspinall, and Lieutenant-Colonel Brudenell White, an Australian on Birdwood's staff. It began for them with the daunting thought that there were close to 85,000 men in the Suvla-Anzac area, plus 2,000 vehicles, 5,000 animals, almost 200 guns and vast piles of stores and ammunition. It was plain that there would be no way of taking all the supplies off, that there would be great losses there. As for the most important commodity, the men, the thought was clear that if a full division and more could be secretly brought ashore as they had been before the August offensive, then it ought to be possible to smuggle men away just as secretly. What was needed was masterly organization and control – something that had not been in evidence at Gallipoli since the very beginning. Now, though, Birdwood's firm hands were at the reins, the incentive was strong and many lessons had been learned. The evacuation machine began to move smoothly.

At first it was felt necessary to keep the real meaning of the preparations secret even from the troops. They were told that the various shifts and moves being made were no more than preparations for the winter. It was a deception impossible to sustain, and the news was universal within days and again engendered a strange contradiction of feelings – a sour anger at the thousands of deaths for no advantage and a slumping relief at having survived so far.

But if the inward deception failed, the outward one began to build towards a remarkable success. The essence of the plan was to maintain a fighting front and, behind it, to siphon men and matériel away so gently, so unobtrusively, that the Turks would not know what was happening. So, through the second and into the third week of December the reverse traffic ran, never appearing to be more than standard back-loading, much of it happening at night, a filter system which moved more than 40,000 men away from Suvla and Anzac in small groups.

The weather improved after the monstrous November blizzard, and there was thin sunshine and a bite in the air, enough to get rid of the flies, not enough to bring shivers. With the added blessing of that fine weather, the complex series of evacuation manoeuvres moved delicately forward, working to a schedule as detailed as any railway timetable:

Unit No.	No. of Men	Begin to Withdraw
5th Aust. Inf. Brigade	1,194	5:20
13th Aust. Light Horse Regt.	310	5:20
29th Indian Brigade	200	8:30
Eastern Mounted Brigade	42	8:30
N.Z. Infantry Brigade	555	8:50
4th Aust. Inf. Brigade	623	9:00
N.Z. Mounted Rifles	509	9:30
1st Aust. Light Horse Bde.	327	9:45
3rd Aust. Light Horse Bde.	160	11:00

And so it went each day. Exact timings were given for the lighters and cutters to take the men out of the waiting ships and precise instructions about the disposition of stores and ammunition, about the movement and loading of horses and mules and vehicles. By the morning of December 18, most of what needed to be done had been done. The force ashore had been reduced quickly and imperceptibly by half, thousands of men slipping down to the beach and the piers in darkness, numbered and coded and moving in quiet lines out to the sea and away – while behind them the men yet to go carried through one of history's great illusions.

It was essential that whatever the Turks saw should give the impression that, if anything other than the normal was going on, it was only part of the preparation for a winter campaign. Allied Intelligence estimated close to 60,000 Turks in the lines at Anzac and Suvla; even an exploration attack could have had the most catastrophic results. So gunfire continued, regular battery tasks in a properly ordered routine; rifles and machine-guns kept firing; wire was renewed and a few conjuring tricks were invented and performed for a very critical audience. Men were instructed to move and loiter in expected places, places which the

A BOOK CREATED UNDER FIRE

In mid-November 1915, under the appalling conditions that were standard for Gallipoli, an enterprise was begun which, perhaps more than any, showed a greatness of spirit. *The Anzac Book* was born — a collection of poems, paintings, cartoons, articles and stories produced by those extraordinary men in the intervals of fighting and surviving.

The introductory note by the book's editor, C.E.W. Bean, stated with eloquent simplicity: "This book of Anzac was produced in the lines at Anzac on Gallipoli in the closing weeks of 1915. Practically every word in it was written and every line drawn beneath the shelter of a waterproof sheet or of a roof of sandbags — either in the trenches or, at most, well within the range of the oldest Turkish rifle, and under daily visitations from the smallest Turkish field-piece. At least one good soldier . . . who was preparing a contribution for these pages, met his death while the work was still unfinished."

All the contributions were produced in the three weeks between November 15 and December 8. "The contributors had to work with such materials as Anzac contained," Bean wrote: "iodine brushes, red and blue pencils, and such approach to white paper as could be produced from each battalion's stationery." And the conditions they worked under were made even more difficult by the two fierce storms that ravaged the peninsula in late November.

The book was produced with the prospect of spending Christmas on Gallipoli, and it was to be published in the new year to help the troops while away the long winter in the trenches. Then came the news that Anzac was to be evacuated. The editing and finishing touches were carried out on the island of Lesbos, and publication was delayed. But, as Bean pointed out, "it was realised by everyone that this production, which was to have been a mere pastime, had now become a hundred times more precious as a souvenir. Certainly no book has ever been produced under these conditions before."

ANZAC FASHIONS. SUMMER

By Bom? R.H.Scott 4th Battery. F.A.

1. Australian sharpshooter disguised as a bush deceives a bird
2. First signs of summer: discarded puttees. Infantryman down from the firing li
3. Water-carrying in hot weather is hard work and requires few clothes
4. Sun-flaps on caps and shorts had quite a good run

LUXURIES FOR THE TURKS

The Ide

And the Real.

COMPLETE SPY OUTFIT FOR SALE.— Including pair of blucher boots, sombrero hat, two cutlasses and a yashmak. Owner having failed to be discovered for two days is going out of business.

SERGT. NOONAN, 6TH BATTN.

MY LADY NICOTINE

(With thanks to all givers of cigarettes)

THE hills of old Gallipoli
　Are barren and austere,
And fairy folk, unhappily,
　Are few indeed out there.

But one I know whose industry
　Both night and day is seen,
For all attest her ministry—
　My Lady Nicotine.

THE HOPELESS DAWN

5. Officer (incog.) armed with stick and bullet-pierced periscope. (No periscope
   is complete without bullet holes testifying to hair-breadth escapes)
6. Gas helmets will never be as popular as home-made shorts
7. The English-made slacks (for the "Australian giants") were much too slack except
   under the armpits
8. Slacks and a roll of blankets give a very Australian appearance

Advertisements

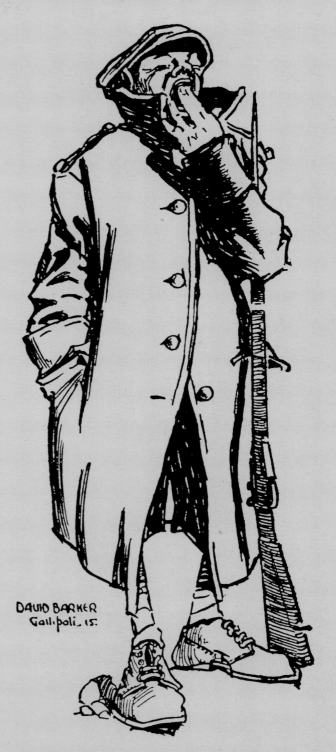

DAVID BARKER
Gallipoli. 15.

"STANDING TO!"—4.30 a.m.

enemy was used to seeing occupied. Trenches were apparently deepened for the winter, although all that was being done was the digging out of soil which was tossed up onto the parapet in plain view – and then allowed to trickle and slide back into the trench.

Outgoing men and beasts and stores went in the night; by daylight empty boxes were unloaded from shore-side boats to make it seem as though supplies were coming in to a beach which was, to all intents and purposes, as crowded and busy as ever. The difficulty was that each morning brought the need for fewer men to appear to be no fewer; each day demanded that action by a diminished number of troops should still have the appearance and the apparent strike-power of the whole mass.

Even the wholesale destruction of stores had to be discreet, what could not be disposed of at night being shuffled away into sheltered corners, boxes and bags dumped into the rocks at the water's edge or buried in gullies or the corners of trenches. Fatigue parties moved about with cans of caustic soda emptying them onto piles of blankets and tarpaulins, onto bags of flour and sugar, piles of stationery, anything that could conceivably be of use to the enemy if left behind. Flour and salt and sugar were also used for another handy purpose; trails of them were laid as guidelines for the men moving down and away in the dark.

The miners and engineers worked below ground till close to the very last, packing the ends of their saps and tunnels with the explosives and ammunition which would not now be used otherwise, running long fuses back and digging the soil down over them to fill the holes and tunnels which had become so familiar. One long tunnel, lined and loaded with explosives, ran out beneath that gruesome spine of land called the Nek.

While the sappers dug destruction into the ground, breakages of all kinds went on above under cover of gunfire – water-pipes were broken, timber strutting put to the axe, even some fires lit and stores burnt. The naval guns fired inshore to supplement the reduced artillery

batteries there, and the wider-spaced men in the trenches moved about to keep the periscopes bobbing and the rifles and machine-guns hot.

This was the time when every ruse and stratagem came into play to fool the Turks, when the floors of trenches, stamped hard by months of use, were dug up to provide a soft and quiet walking surface, when men wrapped rags and socks over their boots before they moved down onto the wooden piers and jetties. And the last of the Gallipoli inventions came into use, the delayed-action rifle. A man would wedge a rifle into a good firing position, load it with one round, cock it and tie an empty tin can by a short length of string to the trigger. A second can, punctured with a small hole and filled with water, would be balanced above the first, and as the water gradually dripped down, the lower can's weight would increase until it was enough to trip the trigger and fire the rifle. There were other devices – machine-guns remotely fired by long stretches of wire and guns fired by weights actuated by candle flames burning slowly through pieces of cord. Enough such things scattered along the firing line gave a fair impression of alert troops.

By the morning of December 19 the forces ashore at Anzac and Suvla had been halved again, 20,000 of them pretending to be four times that number. And still the Turks apparently knew nothing, suspected nothing of the move away. Of all the ploys, perhaps none reassured the enemy more than a group of Australians who spent the better part of an afternoon playing cricket. It must surely have been one of the most unlikely sporting events of all time, those skinny, grimy men cricketing on the open patch of rough ground known as Shell Green (for the appropriate reason that it was under permanent Turkish artillery fire). The shrapnel cut and hissed across the pitch and the outfield, and there was as great a risk of a lost life as of a lost ball.

The timetable went clicking along in a sequence as beautifully ordered as the mechanism of a fine chronometer. Looking back on that December, an observer might properly wonder what the outcome of the Dardanelles campaign would have been if the same forethought and care and precision had been applied earlier, at the landing or at Suvla. Now, when it was all but over, there were no bungling errors, no omissions, no hesitations, nothing but a smooth and delicate tilting of the balance from occupation to evacuation.

On the last night, the night of December 19, the final fine adjustments were made. Earlier that day the Turks had laid down a long and fairly heavy barrage on the beach. But it did not seem to indicate any suspicions on their part; the feeling was that the Turks were merely using up ammunition. Later, in the afternoon, the fleet carried out a very heavy bombardment of the enemy lines at Helles in order to suggest the possibility of an impending attack. A couple of aeroplanes buzzed up and down throughout

most of the daylight hours just to make sure no over-curious German or Turkish planes came on spotting missions.

By a little before nine that night, under a clear and icy moon, barely 5,000 troops held the Anzac lines against an estimated 60,000 Turks. By ten o'clock the staggered and broken front was held by no more than 1,500 men, selected "die-hards", chosen as unlikely to loose their nerves. The final withdrawal began just after 1:30 a.m. when the remaining machine-guns were brought down to the beach. At regular intervals, carefully timed, little groups of six to a dozen men with an officer or senior NCO bringing up the rear came carefully down the tracks and gullies like so many rivulets, coalescing into four lines. They moved quietly, boots muffled, unspeaking, down towards the four embarkation points and onto the sandbag-

The delayed-action rifle devised to help cover the Anzac withdrawal from Gallipoli. Water from the top tin dripped into the lower tin, which pulled the wire and activated the trigger.

THE ANZAC FORCE

During the Dardanelles campaign, soldiers from every Australian state and both islands of New Zealand were in action. Although they made up the bulk of the Australian and New Zealand Army Corps, it is often wrongly assumed that they were the only ones there. In fact, troops from seven countries fought the Turks under the Anzac banner or provided labour forces, as did the group of mule-drivers from India and the 250 volunteers from Palestine – Jewish refugees from pogroms in Russia and Poland. And there were extra labouring tasks carried out by civilians from Malta and Egypt. The troops involved were:

1st ANZAC CORPS
Corps Headquarters
Corps Signals Company
Ceylon Planters' Rifle Corps
Zion Mule Corps
Indian Mule Cart Transport Company
1st Australian Casualty Clearing Station
1st Australian Depot Supply Unit
Beach and fatigue units

Corps Troops
2nd Australian Light Horse Brigade
5th Queensland Regiment
6th New South Wales Regiment
7th New South Wales Regiment

3rd Australian Light Horse Brigade
8th Victoria Regiment
9th Victoria and South Australia Regiment
10th West Australia Regiment

Two Gurkha riflemen take a break from action. Gurkhas of the 29th Indian Infantry Brigade fought bravely with the New Zealanders in the battle for Chunuk Bair.

1st AUSTRALIAN DIVISION
Division Headquarters
Division Artillery: 4th, 5th, 6th, 7th,
8th and 9th Batteries

Divisional Troops
4th Victorian Light Horse Regiment
1st, 2nd and 3rd Companies, Field Engineers
1st, 2nd and 3rd Field Ambulances
Divisional Supply Train

1st Australian Infantry Brigade
1st New South Wales Battalion
2nd New South Wales Battalion
3rd New South Wales Battalion
4th New South Wales Battalion

2nd Australian Infantry Brigade
5th Victoria Battalion
6th Victoria Battalion
7th Victoria Battalion
8th Victoria Ballation

3rd Australian Infantry Brigade
9th Queensland Battalion
10th South Australian Battalion
11th West Australian Battalion
12th South and West Australian and Tasmanian Battalion

2nd AUSTRALIAN DIVISION
Divisional Troops
13th (Victoria) Light Horse Regiment

5th Australian Infantry Brigade
17th New South Wales Battalion
18th New South Wales Battalion
19th New South Wales Battalion
20th New South Wales Battalion

6th Australian Infantry Brigade
21st Victoria Battalion
22nd Victoria Battalion
23rd Victoria Battalion
24th Victoria Battalion

7th Australian Infantry Brigade
25th Queensland Battalion
26th Queensland and Tasmania Battalion
27th South Australia Battalion
28th West Australia Battalion

Gunners of the Kohat Battery of the Indian Mountain Artillery serve a light "screw gun". The guns could be dismantled and carried on mule back to a firing point where they gave support to Anzac troops in forward positions.

Men of the Egyptian labour corps are directed by the military in preparation for their behind-the-lines work of manhandling stores and ammunition. Matériel was landed on Lemnos and then transshipped to Gallipoli.

NEW ZEALAND & AUSTRALIAN DIVISION

Division Headquarters
New Zealand Field Artillery Brigade Headquarters
1 and 2 Batteries Field Artillery

Divisional Troops
New Zealand Field Engineers Company
New Zealand Field Ambulance
4th Australian Field Ambulance
New Zealand and Australian Divisional Supply Train

New Zealand Infantry Brigade
Auckland Battalion
Canterbury Battalion
Otago Battalion
Wellington Battalion

New Zealand Mounted Rifle Brigade
Auckland Mounted Rifles
Canterbury Mounted Rifles
Wellington Mounted Rifles

4th Australian Infantry Brigade
13th New South Wales Battalion
14th Victoria Battalion
15th Queensland and Tasmania Battalion
16th South and West Australian Battalion

1st Australian Light Horse Brigade
1st New South Wales Regiment
2nd Queensland Regiment
3rd South Australian and Tasmanian Regiment

29th Indian Infantry Brigade
14th Sikhs
1st/5th Gurkha Rifles
1st/6th Gurkha Rifles
2nd/10th Gurkha Rifles

ROYAL NAVAL DIVISION

Divisional Troops
No. 1 Field Ambulance
No.1 Field Company, Royal Engineers
No. 2 Field Company, Royal Engineers

Marine Brigade
Chatham Battalion
Portsmouth Battalion

1st Naval Brigade
Nelson Battalion
Deal Battalion

7th Indian Mountain Artillery Brigade
21st (Kohat) Battery
26th (Jacob's) Battery
2nd Indian Field Ambulance
2nd Ammunition Column and Supply Detachment

Maltese labourers stand ready for work at Anzac.

Tracks wind to and fro up Wire Gully to the dugouts and shelters hacked into the scarred hillside.

muffled boards of the jetties. There were motor barges to take them away, 400 to a barge, general and staff officers, sappers and privates and troopers, packed aboard in a tense silence.

The very last men moved back down towards the shore, leaving the rough-hewn holes they had fought from and for those weary months, leaving with a nervous relief, anxious only to get away without being hit, now of all times. For them and for the ones waiting on the barges, it was impossible to forget what they were leaving behind in the chill, musty reek, impossible to forget the dead men who had been their living mates, the hopes of a great victory.

Lone Pine, the dreadful trench-system which had seen the winning of seven Victoria Crosses, was abandoned at 20 minutes to three that icy morning, and the last of the outposts was emptied within three-quarters of an hour, rolls and screens of barbed-wire dragged across the trenches behind the departing men. From 20 kilometres away across the ranges could be heard the rumble and smash of the gunfire at Cape Helles, below the untaken Achi Baba; the British and French down there were to go on fighting for almost another three weeks. At Anzac the water-fired and string-fired and weight-fired guns cracked spasmodically across at the Turkish positions as the last of the last of the Anzacs went down to the beach. Stan Watson, the pier-builder, was among them, and he persuaded the beachmaster to confirm that with an entry in his paybook reading, "Capt. S.H. Watson was the last officer I sent on board at North Beach on the evacuation of Anzac. Signed C.A. Littler, Capt., Beach Commander."

At half-past three the tunnel full of explosives beneath the Nek was detonated, blasting into death more than 60 Turks in a final defiant gesture, their broken bodies mixed with the bones of the Light Horsemen who had charged and fallen and died there. The supply dump on the beach was fired, and the flames licked up into the thin drizzle that had begun to fall. By four o'clock on the morning of December 20, there was not a living Anzac left on Gallipoli.

EVACUATION

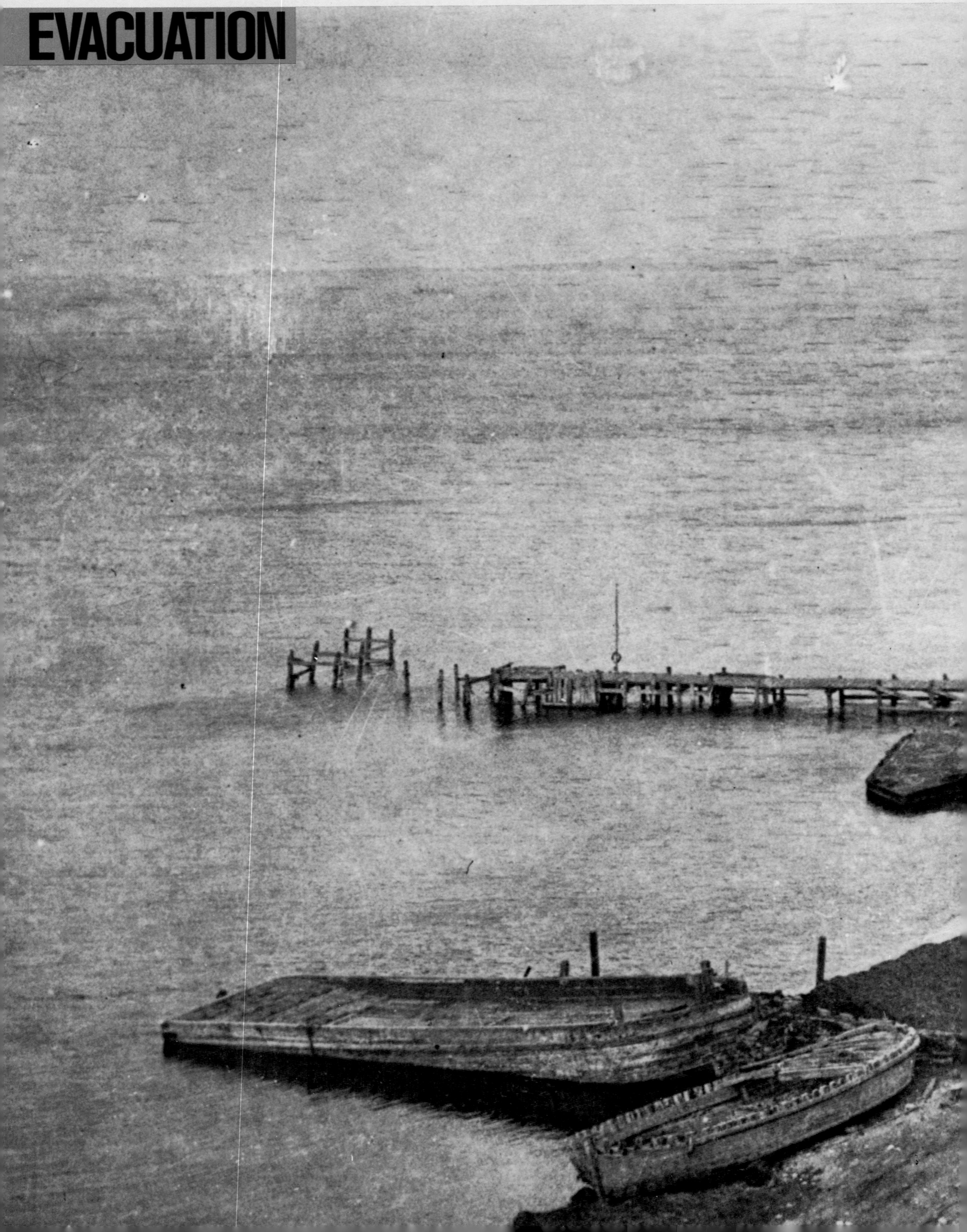

c Beach on December 17, during the last days of the evacuation. Its deserted appearance contrasted sharply with the activity during the night as the troops left.

"To Johnny Turk: We hand over the entire contents of our humble abode"

WITHDRAWAL BY STEALTH

When Lord Kitchener signalled General Bird-wood on December 8, "Cabinet has decided to evacuate positions at Suvla and Anzac at once", a withdrawal plan was already well formed. Evacuation of wounded had, of course, been going on during the whole campaign, casualties being taken to general hospitals on the island of Lemnos. The withdrawal of 40,000 men— more than half of them on the final two nights— was another matter, calling for a degree of organisation that had not been shown before. Under the control of Birdwood and his staff, however, it proved to be the most remarkable exploit of the whole campaign.

Opposite page, top: A string of boats carries wounded soldiers off Gallipoli to a waiting transport. From the first day of the landing, wounded were evacuated to offshore hospitals, ferried out to transports in small boats and lighters. Stretcher cases as well as walking wounded are shown (bottom) being taken aboard the hospital ship Gascon, while those crowded together on wooden bunks (left) look pleased to be leaving Gallipoli.

Anzacs play cricket on Shell Green just before the final evacuation. Activities like these gave the appearance of normality.

Soldiers destroy stores on Anzac Beach in preparation for their departure.

Troops crowd the beachfront at Anzac. It was essential that Anzac Cove look as normal as the Turks had come to expect. Ostensibly, supplies and reinforcements were still coming ashore; most certainly, wounded were still being lifted off right up to the final night of the withdrawal.

A FAREWELL MESSAGE

Much that would have been of value to the Turks was destroyed or rendered useless before the Anzacs stole away. A note left by two soldiers in their home for the past eight months consequently displayed a degree of irony as well as friendliness. It said: "To Johnny Turk: We hand over to you the entire contents of our humble abode. Anything which may benefit you individually you are quite welcome to. You are a fair fighter and deserve all you get. We appreciate the way you have respected the Red Cross."

Above: HMS Cornwallis fires a salvo at the Turks after the evacuation of Anzac and Suvla on December 18-20. The Cornwallis was the last ship to leave Suvla Bay. Right: Burning stores glow in the evening sky.

نعمة رحمنا رنه بخير ووقه رافقة دشنه ناخم ك منقا قبير جهانلميه شاطى ودغمه بريغرين

*Above: Turkish officers on the peak
behind Chunuk Bair survey a deserted
battleground on December 20. Left:
Soldiers pose in front of an Australian
defence position made of sandbags and
ammunition boxes.*

7

GONE AWAY

Over the eight months of the Gallipoli campaign, more than 10,000 Anzacs were killed and another 23,000 were wounded. Those who survived went on to fight on other fronts, maintaining the reputation for courage and endurance earned on Gallipoli.

They had drained away as quietly, as unobtrusively as blood slipping from a severed artery. In that whole secretive spell of three last days and two final nights the thousands of men slid away into safety with barely a handful of them being struck down as they went. Of all the things the months brought to that peninsula of pain and death, none was as remarkable as the leaving of it, defeated in purpose, battered in body, a retreating army leaving its dead on the battlefield yet with a strange new strength and unity and, in the manner of its departure, even a certain dignity. What they had done in that place, the way they did it and the way they left it were to build for them a reputation for great deeds. But at a frightful cost.

There was more than one list of casualty figures produced on each side, and it was perhaps indicative of the generally confused nature of much of the Dardanelles campaign that no one seemed able to bring out a definitive list. Whether one took the lower or the upper calculations, the British, Turkish, German or any of the other figures, the totals were shocking. Averaging them, it seemed that of close to 500,000 Turkish soldiers engaged in the Dardanelles, one in every nine was killed

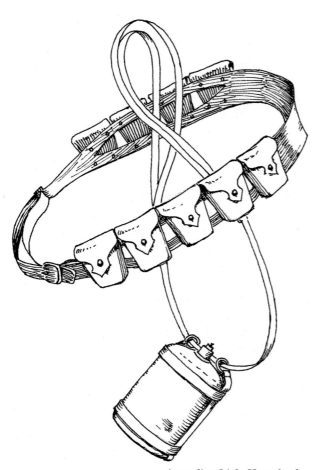

Australian Light Horse leather bandolier and felt-covered water canteen. Each pouch was capable of taking two clips and five rounds of rifle ammunition.

in action and fully half the total force eventually died of wounds and illness – or simply disappeared. The Allies threw into the campaign almost the same number of men, and they lost a little over half: the British, including the Indians and Gurkhas, lost close to 200,000; the French about 30,000. Tiny New Zealand lost almost 7,500, one-third of them dead, and Australian casualties totalled a little more than 26,000, of whom just under 7,600 were killed. A coldly statistical look at those Anzac figures shows that 12 per cent of all Australia's casualties in World War I and 8 per cent of New Zealand's were suffered in eight and a half months on Gallipoli.

There were young men fighting in that campaign whose names were to be famous in later years. The glowingly handsome poet Rupert Brooke died on the way there, fulfilling the prophecy of his sonnet, "If I should die, think only this of me: / That there's some corner of a foreign field / That is for ever England." Clement Attlee, later Prime Minister of England, was – by some accounts – the last British officer away from Cape Helles. The writers Compton Mackenzie and A.P. Herbert served there, the first with the Manchester Regiment, the second with the Royal Naval Division. Bernard Freyberg, who had been one of Brooke's burial party and who had performed most gallantly in the diversion of Bulair on the day of the first landing, went on to earn the Victoria Cross and the Distinguished Service Order with three bars, to command the New Zealanders in the desert and in Italy in World War II and to become Governor-General of New Zealand.

Others who survived that time became notable figures in the new Australia which emerged from the war. The rifle-periscope devised by Corporal W.C. Beech at Quinn's Post was spotted by an Australian major who pressed for its development. The major was called Thomas Blamey, and he was to become his country's first field marshal. There was a young captain in the Warwickshire Regiment who, at Suvla, found himself commanding the battalion because he was the only surviving officer. His name was William Slim, and he too became a field marshal and lived to command an army in Burma and to become a governor-general of Australia. John Monash, a citizen soldier who commanded a brigade at Gallipoli, survived to plan and execute the brilliant and successful tactics of the Battle of Amiens in 1918, when Australian and Canadian troops broke the German line and gained a notable victory.

But no matter what their rank, no matter that most of them achieved no national or international fame, all of the men who came through the ordeal of Gallipoli were changed in some manner. The ones who came away were different, not just different in themselves, not only changed from what they had been, but different from other men. They had endured almost insufferable privations with stoicism and gallantry and had retained enough of humanity in bestial circumstances to show compassion and even humour. Enough examples of both those things can be seen in the contributions to *The Anzac Book*. Ernest Hemingway described courage as "grace under pressure", and that serves well to sum up the Anzacs in the Dardanelles. But because the were forced to, they became different. They became harder.

No ordinary man goes day after day, month after month, in the immediate presence of violent death without being affected. Gallipoli was a crucible which took the simple elements of the young Australians of that time and caused them to melt and run and fuse into a tougher metal. The men who went home at last had lost some gentleness from their past, lost some sympathy for things which they saw as inessential; they had lost some degree of tolerance perhaps, especially for people who had not been down into the pit they had known. It was almost a form of snobbery, the sort of élitism which has always existed among soldiers who have suffered greatly together and survived. The survivors of a shipwreck or an earthquake have the same sort of bond.

With the Anzacs of Gallipoli there was something extra. Every man of them was a volunteer, had gone of his own free will into that

FOR VALOUR: THE VICTORIA CROSS

It is a plain, almost sombre, medal. Queen Victoria instituted it as the Empire's highest decoration for bravery in battle. That was in 1856, the year that saw the end of the Crimean War, the key battle in which was the eleven-month-long siege of Sevastopol. Among the military plunder and souvenirs taken back to Britain by her victorious regiments were a number of Russian guns captured when Sevastopol fell, and the Victoria Cross was first cast in bronze from those guns, a tradition that persisted for almost a century. To wear the bronze cross on the simple deep red ribbon is to be seen as among the bravest of the brave. The inscription says it all—"For Valour."

Ten Anzacs were awarded the Victoria Cross during the Gallipoli campaign, fully one quarter of the total. And while nine went to Australians and one to a New Zealander, that fact cannot be seen to reflect greater and lesser levels of bravery. Nor can it truly be said that those who won the Victoria Cross were the bravest of the brave; it is without doubt that there were hundreds of individual acts of courage that went unnoticed and unrewarded. The Victoria Cross men were seen to show valour and were recommended by superior officers or, under the unique privilege that attaches to this award, were elected to become recipients by the members of their units.

Lance-Corporal Albert Jacka, aged 22. Jacka was the first Australian to be awarded the Victoria Cross in World War I. At Courtney's Post during the Turkish attack on May 19-20, he leapt alone into a section of trench taken by the Turks, shot five, bayoneted two more and forced the rest to abandon the captured trench.

Lance-Corporal L.M. Keysor, aged 19. At Lone Pine on August 7, Keysor picked up two live Turkish bombs and threw them back at the enemy. Although wounded, he kept throwing bombs—both Turkish and the crude Australian type fabricated on the beach—for 50 hours before consenting to be evacuated for medical treatment.

Corporal Cyril Bassett, aged 23. The only member of the New Zealand forces to be awarded a Victoria Cross during the Gallipoli campaign, Bassett received the award for his action as a signaller establishing and maintaining communications under fire in the battle at Chunuk Bair on August 8.

Lieutenant William Symons, aged 26. At Lone Pine on the night of August 8-9, he was in command of a newly captured section of trench and repelled several counter-attacks. He led a charge that drove the Turks out of an isolated sap, killed two with his pistol, then drove off further attacks by the enemy.

Captain Frederick Tubb, aged 33. During the Turkish counter-attack at Lone Pine on August 9, Tubb commanded a section of trench that saw some furious fighting. Three times he led his men back to drive off the Turks and rebuild a sandbag barricade blown in by the enemy, during which he was wounded in the head.

Corporal Alexander Burton, aged 22. Burton was posthumously awarded the Victoria Cross for his actions at Lone Pine on August 9, where he was killed by an exploding bomb as he was rebuilding a barricade with Captain Tubb and Corporal Dunstan after repelling the Turks for the third time from their sap.

Corporal William Dunstan, aged 20. Dunstan was the third member, with Tubb and Burton, of the group who were each awarded the Victoria Cross for their actions in driving off the enemy and rebuilding the trench barricade at Lone Pine. He was temporarily blinded by the bomb that killed Burton during their action.

Captain A.J. Shout, aged 33. On August 9, during the battle at Lone Pine, Shout and another officer made a series of charges down a sap to clear it, one bombing, the other shooting. Shout killed eight Turks and routed the remainder before a bomb exploded in his hand. He died of his wounds two days later.

Private John Hamilton, aged 19. When the Turks forced the barricade at Sasse's sap during a counter-attack at Lone Pine on August 9, Hamilton lay out on the parapet and shouted directions to the bomb throwers in the trenches while keeping up a constant sniping fire against the Turkish bombers, who were driven off.

Lieutenant Hugo Throssell, aged 30. Throssell was awarded the Victoria Cross for conspicuous bravery during the capture of Hill 60 on August 29-30. Despite terrible wounds, he refused to leave his post for medical assistance until all danger passed, and then returned to the firing line when his wounds had been dressed.

cauldron. Even a broad simplicity, a general lack of knowledge about all the factors involved, cannot diminish their willingness to serve.

Herbert Asquith, who had been Prime Minister of Britain throughout the Dardanelles campaign, made a statement to the House of Commons in March 1917, with the war still raging. He was referring to the report of the Dardanelles Commission, which had sat for more than a year to consider the conduct of the campaign. Asquith said, in part, that "to describe the expedition as a tragedy and a catastrophe was a complete perversion of the case. I boldly claim that it absolutely saved the position of Russia in the Caucasus, delayed for months the defection of Bulgaria, kept at least 300,000 Turks immobilised and was one of the contributory causes of the favourable development of events in Egypt, Mesopotamia and Persia."

Both German and Turkish commanders and senior officers made it plain after the events that there were times when only the smallest extra push would have seen a breakthrough and the Allies on the way to Constantinople. Twice they had considered pulling back from Achi Baba; at Suvla, at Chunuk Bair, the balance was absolutely level and could have been tipped with that added thrust, and the temptation is always there to conjecture at the shape of today's world if the Anzacs had succeeded in their task. Instead they came away from the carnage and, tired, sick and damaged as they were, became a solid base, a bedrock on which was built another army who were yet to fight – successfully – in France and Flanders and across the deserts to Gaza and Beersheba and Damascus.

There was, after Gallipoli, a reputation to maintain, a certain standing in the eyes of the world. They had established themselves as tough men, as men who could endure; they could fight and go on fighting no matter what;

and even if they were beaten, it was never for lack of courage or stamina or spirit. They were something special. They became the core of the Anzac legend, the heart centre of the soldiers from Down Under in Australia and New Zealand – often reckless and undisciplined, except in action; not much given to passing military courtesies, except where their officers had proved themselves; ready to fight anyone, except their mates. Some few of the Gallipoli men stayed healthy enough and were tough enough to force back the desolate memories or to look at them newly and to go again twenty years later to another war. The reputation won in the Dardanelles stood intact then and again, later, in the Middle East and New Guinea, and in Malaya and Korea and Vietnam.

The name Gallipoli is a battle honour on flags and drums and pennants in many places of the world. There are newly merged County regiments of Britain which have inherited the colours of old and defunct battalions that fought there; in far parts of India and Pakistan and Nepal, military establishments still house crests and banners with "Gallipoli" lettered in gold on them, as do the ante-rooms of regimental messes in France. In the place itself, on that dread peninsula, almost 11,000 Allied dead lie buried; over 30,000 more lie in unknown graves deep in the thyme-heavy gullies and beneath the jagged slopes, in company with the thousands of unburied Turkish dead.

There were many medals won for bravery and devotion to duty in the Dardanelles. But – and perhaps this is a reflection of the grimness of the place and what went on there – neither Germany nor Turkey, neither Britain nor France, neither New Zealand nor Australia struck a campaign medal for the men who fought there. No military medal bears the campaign clasp "Gallipoli".

The expression on the face of Regimental Sergeant-Major Melville of the 1st Battalion, photographed on August 15, 1915, reflects the strain of existence for the soldier on Gallipoli. The white identification armbands were worn when going into action.

BIBLIOGRAPHY

Adam-Smith, Patsy. *The Anzacs.* Melbourne: Nelson, 1978.

All-Australia Memorial, The. British-Australasian Publishing Service, 1917.

Barnett, Corelli. *The Great War.* London: Peerage Books, 1979.

Bean, C.E.W. *Anzac to Amiens.* Canberra: Australian War Memorial, 1946.

————.*Official History of Australia in the War of 1914-1918.* Sydney: Angus & Robertson, 1921-43.

Bell, A.D., ed. *An Anzac's War Diary: The Story of Sergeant Richardson.* Adelaide: Rigby, 1980.

Bishop, Edward. *Better to Die.* London; New England Library, 1976.

Bush, Eric. *Gallipoli.* London: Allen & Unwin, 1975.

Churchill, Winston S. *The World Crisis.* London: Butterworth, 1923.

Denham, H.M. *Dardanelles: A Midshipman's Diary, 1915-16.* London: John Murray, 1981.

Falls, Cyril, ed. *Great Military Battles.* London: Weidenfeld & Nicolson, 1964.

Firkins, Peter. *The Australians in Nine Wars.* Adelaide: Rigby, 1971.

Gallishaw, John. *Trenching At Gallipoli.* New York: A.L. Burt, 1916.

Gammage, Bill. *The Broken Years.* Canberra: Australian National University Press, 1974.

Hamilton, Sir Ian. *Gallipoli Dispatches.* London: HMSO, 1916.

Hargrave, John. *The Suvla Bay Landing.* London: Macdonald, 1964.

Hart, Liddell, *History of the World War.* London: Faber, 1934.

James, Robert Rhodes. *Gallipoli.* Sydney: Angus & Robertson, 1965.

Kannengiesser, Hans. *The Campaign in Gallipoli.* London: Hutchinson, 1917.

Laffin, John. *"Damn the Dardanelles!": The Story of Gallipoli.* Sydney: Doubleday Australia, 1980.

McCarthy, Dudley. *Gallipoli to the Somme: The Story of C.E.W. Bean.* Sydney: John Ferguson, 1983.

McKernan, Michael. *The Australian People and the Great War.* Melbourne: Nelson, 1980.

Masefield, John. *Gallipoli.* London: Heinemann, 1916.

Mitchell, Elyne. *Light Horse.* Melbourne: Macmillan Australia, 1978.

Moorehead, Alan. *Gallipoli.* London: Hamish Hamilton, 1956.

Nevinson, Henry. *The Dardanelles Campaign.* London: Nisbet, 1918.

North, John. *Gallipoli: The Fading Vision.* London: Faber, 1934.

Pearl, Cyril, *Anzac Newsreel: A Picture History of Gallipoli.* Sydney: Ure Smith, 1963.

Pictures of the Battlefields of Anzac, by the War Correspondent of the *Age.* Melbourne: Osboldstone, 1916.

Pugsley, Christopher. *Gallipoli: The New Zealand Story.* Auckland: Hodder & Stoughton, 1984.

Reid, John B. *Australian Artists at War.* Melbourne: Sun Books, 1977.

Swifte, Tim. *Gallipoli: The Incredible Campaign.* Sydney: Magazine Promotions, 1985.

Uluaslan, Hüseyin. *Gallipoli Campaign.* Canakkale, Turkey, 1986.

Waite, Fred. *The New Zealanders at Gallipoli.* Christchurch: Whitcombe & Tombs, 1921.

Watson, Stan H. 'Gallipoli: The Tragic Truth'. Typescript.

Wigmore, Lionel, with Bruce Harding, revised by Jeff Williams and Anthony Staunton. *They Dared Mightily.* Canberra: Australian War Memorial, 1986.

ACKNOWLEDGMENTS

For their help in the preparation of this book, the publishers wish to thank the director and staff of the Australian War Memorial, Canberra: Air Vice-Marshal J. H. Flemming (director), Dr Michael McKernan (assistant director), Brian Butler, George Imashev, Ian Affleck, Steve Corvini, Andrew Jack, Peter West, Beryl Strusz and Anne Gray. The publishers also thank Virginia Eddy, Features Services, John Fairfax and Sons Ltd; Bob Leonard of Westpac Banking Corporation; Phillip Tardif, for permission to use extracts from the diary of Leslie Lott; and Ruth Funder, Stella Guthrie, Galli Ripka, Warwick Sharpe, the late Lieutenant-Colonel L. B. Swift, and the Watson family.

PICTURE CREDITS

Credits from left to right are separated by semicolons, from top to bottom by oblique strokes. AWM = Australian War Memorial.

COVER and page 1: AWM A2022.

THE DARDANELLES: STRUGGLE AT SEA. 6: Drawing by Charles Goodwin. 8: Courtesy Westpac. 9, 10: Maps by Wendy Gorton.

THE CHANCE OF A LIFETIME. 12, 13: AWM A3406. 4: John Fairfax and Sons Ltd. 15: AWM V7626 / State Library of Victoria. 16, 17: John Fairfax and Sons Ltd / John Fairfax and Sons Ltd; John Fairfax and Sons Ltd; AWM V417. 18: Courtesy Warwick Sharpe, Sydney / AWM V5136 / John Fairfax and Sons Ltd. 19: State Library of Victoria; AWM V26 / AWM J340. 20: Courtesy Warwick Sharpe, Sydney / Mitchell Library. 21: Courtesy L.L. Sawyer, Sydney; AWM 4118 / AWM J1605.

THE LAND AND THE LANDING. 22: Drawing by Charles Goodwin. 25: AWM G549. 26: AWM G2066 / AWM G894. 27: AWM A3362 / AWM G1222. 28, 29: John Fairfax and Sons Ltd. 30, 31: Drawings by Charles Goodwin.

GETTING ASHORE. 34,35: AWM A1829. 36: AWM A2468. 37: John Fairfax and Sons Ltd; AWM A1148. 38, 39: John Fairfax and Sons Ltd. 40: AWM G903 / AWM J3022. 41: Courtesy Mr and Mrs Steel, Auckland. 42: AWM C964. 43: AWM G907 / AWM G918. 44: AWM G915. 45: AWM A3869.

THE ENEMY FACE. 46, 47: Courtesy Westpac. 48,49: John Fairfax and Sons Ltd. 50: John Fairfax and Sons Ltd. 51, 52: Courtesy Westpac. 53: AWM A2598. 54: AWM G271 / G456. 55–57: Courtesy Westpac.

LIVING HARD, DYING HARD. 58: Drawing by Charles Goodwin. 60. AWM 1011; AWM J6792. 62: Map by Wendy Gorton. 63: AWM A1506 / AWM H3954. 65: John Fairfax and Sons Ltd. 66: AWM G518 / AWM G766 / Courtesy Warwick Sharpe, Sydney.

HOME WAS NEVER LIKE THIS. 68, 69: AWM G320. 70, 71: AWM A907; AWM G408 / AWM A830. 72: AWM C1872 / AWM C3374. 73: AWM G579 / AWM G268. 74,

75: AWM 6544. 76: AWM A5291; AWM C1761 / AWM G599. 77: AWM C3420. 78: AWM G401 / AWM G269 / John Fairfax and Sons Ltd. 79: AWM A5401 / AWM G762; State Library of Victoria / AWM C3611.

SPRING AND SUMMER SLAUGHTER. 80: Drawing by Charles Goodwin. 82: Courtesy Mrs Ruth Funder, Melbourne; AWM H3953. 83: AWM C3391 / *The Changing of the Guard*, published by the AWM. 85: AWM A847. 86, 87: AWM G1960. 88,89: Courtesy Mr and Mrs Steel, Auckland; John Fairfax and Sons Ltd / AWM G302; Courtesy Mr and Mrs Steel, Auckland. 91: AWM A2022. 92: AWM A2055. 94, 95: AWM C199.

THE ARTISTS' WAR. 97: AWM 22. 98: AWM 2838. 99: AWM 2873 / AWM 7965. 100, 101: AWM 2161. 102: *The Anzac Book*. 103: AWM 3221 / AWM 3227. 104: AWM 5000. 105: AWM.

AUTUMN MADNESS. 106: Drawing by Charles Goodwin. 109: AWM A1520. 110: AWM A2156E. 111: Map by Wendy Gorton. 113: AWM A5396; AWM A5382. 115: AWM G528 / AWM A3549. 116, 117: AWM H3951; Courtesy Mr and Mrs Steel, Auckland. 118: AWM A2026.

THE HOME FRONT. 120, 121: AWM H11613. 122, 123: John Fairfax and Sons Ltd. 124: AWM Special Collections. 125: AWM Special Collections / Mitchell Library. 126–130: John Fairfax. 131: Courtesy Westpac; AWM H11576 / AWM H11575; Courtesy Westpac. 132, 133: John Fairfax and Sons Ltd.

THE WICKED WIND OF WINTER. 134: Drawing by Charles Goodwin. 136, 137: AWM G573. 138: AWM G1231. 140: AWM G1267 / AWM C2193. 142, 143: *The Anzac Book*. 145: AWM G1291. 146: AWM C1720 / AWM C2073. 147: AWM C4643 / AWM C3561.

EVACUATION. 150, 151: AWM G1287. 152: AWM A1798 / AWM A2740. 153: AWM C1788. 154, 155: AWM G1289 / AWM G1276; AWM PS1659. 156, 157: AWM G658; Courtesy Westpac / AWM A3312; Courtesy Westpac.

GONE AWAY. 158: Drawing by Charles Goodwin. 160: AWM B5255 / AWM A2868; AWM D21 / AWM H15475; AWM H6206. 161: AWM H6786; AWM H6785; AWM H6201 / AWM G1028; AWM J3071; AWM A3688.

INDEX

Numerals in italics indicate an
illustration of the subject mentioned.

S4
3115